THE COMMONWEALTH AND INTERNATIONAL LIBRARY

Joint Chairmen of the
Honorary Editorial Advisory Board
SIR ROBERT ROBINSON, O.M., F.R.S.,
London
and DEAN ATHELSTAN SPILHAUS,
Minnesota

Publisher   ROBERT MAXWELL, M.C., M.P.

PSYCHOLOGY DIVISION

General Editor   PROF. G. P. MEREDITH

PRINCIPLES
OF TRAINING

A

PRINCIPLES
OF TRAINING

D. H. HOLDING
M.A., Ph.D.

Department of Psychology,
University of Leeds.

PERGAMON PRESS

OXFORD · LONDON · EDINBURGH · NEW YORK
PARIS · FRANKFURT

Pergamon Press Ltd., Headington Hill Hall, Oxford
4 & 5 Fitzroy Square, London W.1

Pergamon Press (Scotland) Ltd., 2 & 3 Teviot Place, Edinburgh 1

Pergamon Press Inc., 122 East 55th Street, New York 22, N.Y.

Pergamon Press GmbH, Kaiserstrasse 75, Frankfurt-am-Main

Federal Publications Ltd., Times House, River Valley Rd., Singapore

Samcax Book Services Ltd., Queensway, P.O. Box 2720, Nairobi, Kenya

Library of Congress Catalog Card No. 65-18377

First edition 1965

Printed in Great Britain by
A. Brown & Sons Ltd., Hull, London and Northampton

CONTENTS

CONTENTS

EDITOR'S INTRODUCTION

It is probably true to say that training is as old as civilization, if not older. Certainly today we can see training schemes multiplying at a prodigious rate in most parts of the world, both in countries moving on to more advanced systems of technology and in those struggling to catch up with existing systems. (Here I use the term "technology" in the widest sense to refer to the theories and techniques for dealing with the machinery not only of industry but also of agriculture, commerce, administration, military activity, medicine, communication and education. We even see technology creeping into the arts, into scholarship, into law and into politics itself.) In all these fields new skills have to be mastered and everywhere the problem of devising efficient training schemes has to be faced. In the past this problem has not always been well defined. The possession of a skill is no guarantee of an ability to pass it on to others. Too often the schemes have amounted to little more than "sitting by Nellie". Even when carefully thought out and well organized they often rest on a set of tacit psychological assumptions which are quite untested, and which, indeed, the authors might well be at a loss to know how to test.

We have here, then, a field for applied psychology in which far too little psychology has been applied. And it is a field of world-wide interest and importance. It comes as a challenge to psychology and as a temptation. It is a challenge to find the right answers. It is a temptation to claim that we know them all already. It is a temptation to which psychologists have been showing an increasing and welcome resistance. As a psychologist myself I am constantly amazed by what I am supposed to assume to know. The public do not really believe that the psychologist is a magician, but they show in many ways that they think he believes himself to be one. Yet nearly always when it comes to a concrete question involving the judgement of intelligence, of character, of skill, it is the "man-in-the-street" who is sure of his own verdict. The psychologist says, "We can't know without testing."

In techniques of training, we find the experienced trainer often overconfident of the superiority of his particular methods—more by reason of his own facility in handling them than from any demonstrated comparison with alternative methods. And when it is a question of designing *new* training schemes for new skills it is all too easy to imitate techniques which have worked well enough for other (sometimes quite different) skills, rather than to submit the new skill to a fundamental analysis and ask what *known* fundamental principles are relevant to its mastery. The reluctance to attempt this more difficult task derives probably from two sources.

(1) The fact that we have, in fact, no sufficiently well-tested, agreed and codified *system* of principles of training:-

(2) The fact that we have no clearly thought out and scientifically validated system for *training the trainers* (in spite of a century or more of teacher-training schemes).

These two deficiencies are clearly related.

There are plenty of systems of teacher-training, based mainly on traditional philosophies of education, a smattering of arbitrarily selected psychological findings and a miscellany of rule-of-thumb recipes. The thought needed to drag teacher-training, kicking and screaming, into the twentieth century is dissipated in the interminable and self-stultifying debates among academic educationists at annual conferences on "educational issues". And unfortunately the constructive addition which experimental psychology *could* make towards a positive outcome is cancelled by the *subtractive* consequence of half a century of psychometric endeavours to provide excuses for not attempting to see how far children can respond to good teaching. Thus the educationist's image of psychology is darkened by ambiguity.

A radically new chapter of educational psychology is needed to direct into educational thought not merely the laboratory *findings* of experimental psychology (indeed, as appears from Dr. Holding's book, the concrete findings themselves, taken in isolation, may often seem too restricted for direct educational application) but, more positively, the analytical insight into perceptual, operational and communicative processes, the strategy and design of experiments, the quantitative precision, the functional conceptualization, the awareness of multiple variation and individual differences and the sheer technical "know-how" of investigation.

One of the merits of Dr. Holding's book is that it demonstrates the conditions for the application of psychological findings. Even when a fairly definite conclusion emerges from a series of experiments this cannot be assumed to apply over an unrestricted range of training situations. The point is well illustrated on page 92 with regard to speed and accuracy. The relation between these factors necessarily depends on the nature of the task. Hence an awareness of experimental findings must be paralleled by competence in analysing tasks in order to determine how and where any particular principles may reasonably be applied. By covering such a wide sample of experimental data this book reveals to the intending practitioner of training, whether in industry, in sport, in the defence services or other fields, the extent of the problem of analysis. The actual findings of an experiment may well vary from one group of subjects to another and from one set of physical equipment to another. The findings nevertheless represented a particular, limited truth which has more substance to it than mere opinion. More importantly it is a statement whose terms have a precise empirical meaning because it has been demonstrated in defined physical conditions. Numerical scores and statistical inferences may vary as the physical conditions and the human capacities alter quantitatively in different situations, but if the tasks remain structurally similar the experimental statements retain clear meanings.

No experimental psychologist would claim that his findings have unrestricted application. The important contribution made by this book should therefore be seen to lie in the greatly enhanced insight which it yields into the variables presented by any training task.

On a first reading of this book the enthusiast for applied science may well find his ardour somewhat damped. For although the author would not claim, within the compass of one short book, to have exhausted the whole field of well-attested findings from all researches on training up to date, he would, I think, regard his sample as a fair indication of "the state of the art". In other words those who feel that they cannot embark on the design of any new training scheme unless they have scientific assurance from experimental findings in psychology that their scheme is the best possible, may well find Dr. Holding's caution inhibitory. Their discouragement represents a rather widespread misconception of the nature of applied science and, in particular, of the way to interpret experiments. There is a tendency to put all the emphasis on the *result* of the experiment and to miss the significance of a large mass of information implicit in the description of the experimental procedure. The result of an experiment is critically dependent on the sample of subjects and materials used, on the variables chosen for measurement and the instruments used for measuring them, on the details of the experimental design and on the conceptual framework behind the formulae applied. The description of the experiment carries important information quite apart from the particular measured outcome. In analysing the variables involved in a particular skill, and in the training for that skill, the experimenter is performing an essential service for anyone responsible for designing a training scheme. It is very unlikely that the persons and materials to whom his scheme will be applied will precisely correspond in type or quantity with those used in the experiment, nor are the working conditions likely to be the same. Thus the actual measured outcome of the experiment may well be the least significant information which it provides. The experiment demonstrates two things: first that a certain procedure is feasible, and second that it can be precisely analysed as a system of variables. In addition the actual experimentation commonly demands the exercise of a good deal of ingenuity and inventiveness in the instrumentation, the preparation of the materials, the handling of the subjects and the conduct of the operations. All this is sheer gain and if the experiment is adequately reported and illustrated any reader closely concerned with designing a scheme of his own stands to benefit enormously by all this "information fall-out"—so long as he is not so obsessed by the numerical outcome that he misses the significance of the process by which it was reached.

These considerations hold good widely beyond the bounds of applied psychology—indeed one might claim that their fuller appreciation would benefit the whole of technology. For however "pure" a scientific specialist may regard himself, the carrying out of any experimental research is a good deal more than an exercise in logic. It is almost always an occasion for technical innovation. The inventions of the research-worker are often hidden away in the recesses of his apparatus or wrapped up in his formulae, unacknowledged, unpatented and unreported. Beyond being particular solutions to particular problems their potentiality for generalization may escape his notice. If the report is sufficiently detailed, other research-workers may pick up their scientific significance, but their value as technical innovations may still be overlooked. How much of the fruit of originality is going to waste in this way no one can say, but the mere possibility suggests that there is more than one way of reading a scientific report. It also suggests that many experiments may actually go unreported because they have yielded negative or disappointing results. What is thus lost is not merely a result but an analysis, a design and an invention.

The bearing of this on the relation between research and development is obvious. Development, in the broad sense of the application of research to technical improvements, is a constructive, creative process in which scientific facts are translated into materializations. But the facts are more than the experimental results. They are the whole content of the experiment.

As a science, modern psychology is not only quantitative but empirical, conceptual and pragmatic. Today it involves increasingly elaborate assemblies of technical equipment, professional skills and laboratory space. It also requires an understanding and appreciative clientèle to apply and benefit by what it has to offer. This offering is not a set of cut-and-dried conclusions but a whole vital chapter of science, the chapter dealing with the human variable in natural phenomena. In a series of publications devoted to presenting the kind of psychology needed both for the assertion of human needs and ends, and for the demonstration of the technical means for fulfilling these in the years immediately ahead, it is not inappropriate to open with a modest statement of ascertained data in the field of training. For it will be, above all, on an increasingly adequate supply of personnel, trained in all kinds of novel skills and approaches, that our successful adaptation to the new man-made environment, without sacrificing the irreplaceable patterns of the natural environment, will depend. We need to recultivate both the industrial waste-land bequeathed to us by nineteenth-century technology and the intellectual waste-land created by twentieth-century philosophy. As this editor sees it this task of recivilizing ourselves will be achieved neither by a purely economic emphasis on mechanical efficiency, nor by a purely abstract debate on words and principles, but by the scrupulous attention to persons and processes which characterizes the training of the experimental psychologist. This is a hope, not yet an attested claim, and it will be for subsequent volumes in this series to indicate the concepts and the means for fulfilling this hope.

Leeds   PATRICK MEREDITH
   January 1965

ACKNOWLEDGEMENTS

The following acknowledgements and thanks are due to

The American Journal of Psychology for permission to reproduce a figure and data from their journal. (Figs. 29 and 31.)

The American Psychological Association for permission to reproduce diagrams from *Psychological Monographs*. (Figs. 11 and 12.)

The American Psychological Association and the authors, where they could be traced, for permission to reproduce diagrams from the *Journal of Experimental Psychology*. (Figs. 5, 9, 21, 25, 27, 28 and 30.)

The American Psychological Association and J. O. Cook for permission to reproduce diagrams from the *American Psychologist*. (Figs. 35 and 37.)

The American Psychological Association and L. T. Alexander for permission to reproduce a graph from the *Journal of Applied Psychology*. (Fig. 8.)

The British Psychological Society for permission to use data from the *British Journal of Psychology*. (Figs. 3, 15, 17 and 33.)

W. Heffer and Son Ltd. and J. Annett for permission to reproduce a graph from the *Quarterly Journal of Experimental Psychology*. (Fig. 6.)

Houghton Mifflin Company for permission to reprint a diagram from the *Handbook of Psychological Research on the Rat* (Munn). (Fig. 10.)

The Institute of Personnel Management and the author for permission to reprint the graph from *Operator Training in Industry* (Seymour). (Fig. 1.)

The Journal Press, Massachusetts, for permission to reproduce data from the *Journal of General Psychology*. (Figs. 2, 12 and 21.)

ACKNOWLEDGEMENTS

The National Education Association of Washington for permission to reproduce a diagram from *Teaching Machines and Programmed Learning—A Source Book*, 1960. (Fig. 34.)

The National Institute of Industrial Psychology and the author for permission to use data from *Occupational Psychology*, the journal of the Institute (by arrangement with the editor).

The publishers of *Perceptual and Motor Skills* and P. D. McCormack for permission to reproduce a graph from the journal. (Fig. 32.)

Taylor and Francis Ltd. for permission to reproduce certain figures from *Ergonomics* and to use data from that journal. (Figs. 13, 14, 16, 18, 19, 23 and 24.)

In addition, thanks are due to Mrs. B. McLumpha and to Mr. M. R. Lee for their work in preparing these illustrations.

1. INTRODUCTION

EVERYONE undergoes training. We learn to walk, to swim or to ride a bicycle; we learn to speak a foreign language, to do arithmetic or to read a map; and we learn to do a job in a factory, an office or a laboratory, in a variety of occupations. In most of these cases someone else is arranging the conditions in which we practise and learn.

A parent, a teacher, an instructor or a trainer *will tell us what to do and what to expect. He will provide the equipment and watch how we use it. He may guide our movements, or perhaps let us try out a word or an action and then show where we went wrong. He will give us hints on how to cope with the awkward parts. He will encourage us to practise and let us know whether we have improved, or how we stand up to comparison with other people.* All these things are part of what we call "training" and may be done well or badly.

It is easy to see why we tend to call these activities "training" and not "education". In all these examples we are trying to learn, or teach, quite specific skills. The object of a *training* scheme may be stated quite explicitly and the methods used should give measurable results. In *education* on the other hand the aims of our teaching are broader, and we may even take a pride in the fact that our procedures are not demonstrably efficient. Quite often we assume that our teaching will have its effect in a development of mental processes which will stand the student in good stead in later life, the results being spread over too wide a range of activities for direct measurement to be successful.

In fact, many of the problems of education are those concerned with deciding what kind of effect we are trying to produce, whereas the problems of training lie in discovering the most effective means

of achieving specified results, as in teaching welding or gymnastics
Of course training and education overlap and there are many border-
line cases. We have already mentioned learning a foreign language.
This often takes place in school and we tend to associate it with
education, since we may be learning Latin, or German or French,
for no particular purpose. It might be argued that this ambiguity of
purpose has made language teaching in schools less efficient than it
might otherwise be when treated simply as a training problem.
Certainly if we genuinely wish to speak a foreign language very
effective training methods are available. There will be an opportunity to examine these methods in a later chapter.

EVALUATION OF TRAINING

Since our objectives in training may be clearly stated there is no
need to carry out our training "blind". There is little justification
for a training programme which is not known to work. Mere
opinions are not good enough since these are often more favourable
than is warranted by the recorded results. Nevertheless, in a survey
of 237 industrial training schemes undertaken by the National Institute of Industrial Psychology (1956) figures for training effectiveness,
in terms of the amount by which learning time was reduced by the
schemes, could be supplied in only 24 cases.

Finding out whether training works can be done quite systematically if records are kept, by examining changes in the scores for
performance on the task, or by building up graphs which show the
course of learning. An example is provided by an industrial study
carried out by Seymour (1959). In Fig. 1 we can see that he has been
able to present several kinds of information. The lower curve shows
the gradual improvement, over a period of twelve weeks, of a group
of operators who learned the task in an unsystematic way by
"picking it up" on the shop floor. From the upper curve we can
see the effects of a formal training scheme. Notice that this group,
after only three weeks of formal training, begin at a level of skill
which was only reached by the lower group after twelve weeks.
Further, although there is some rise in the upper curve after the end
of the training period it is clear that the training scheme has brought
these operators very close to their final limit of performance.

In any training situation we may reasonably ask whether our

methods have resulted in any improvement of skill, or in making it easier or quicker to acquire the skill, and whether one method gives more improvement than another. In this we are in a similar position to the learner. He too must know what he is trying to do and how far he has managed to achieve it, if he is to make any progress. This is probably best seen in terms of a concrete example.

Let us take the case of learning to aim a rifle at a distant target. There is no point in loosing off shots at the target if there is no way of telling where the bullets went. It is true that the learner will

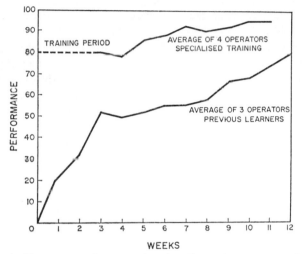

Fig. 1. Factory records comparing the effects of systematic training with learning by experience. From Seymour (1959).

gain some benefit from getting accustomed to the noise and the recoil, but his aim will improve no further unless he can see the holes in the target or unless the score is signalled back. In order to improve in a trial-and-error situation he must have "knowledge of results".

So it is with the trainer. There is no point in setting up a training programme, particularly an expensive and lengthy programme, without trying to evaluate its results. Preferably one should evaluate separately all the parts which make up the training programme. Given this kind of detailed information we may begin to look for ways of adjusting our methods. In order to make adjustments we can bring to bear a great deal of established knowledge on training techniques, of the kind discussed in later chapters.

EXPERIMENTS ON TRAINING

In order to clarify the problems of training we shall have to call upon a great deal of evidence from experimental psychology. This may not require justification, although it is not widely known how far psychologists have concerned themselves with straightforward problems of learning and training—problems of the analysis of skills, the conditions of practice, the effects of knowledge of results and kindred problems which the trainer must face in his work. Psychology is in fact the experimental study of behaviour, particularly *human behaviour*; and out of the many experimental studies carried out in applied learning situations, particularly since the war, a great deal of new knowledge has been amassed.

The persistent public image of the psychologist as a mysterious eccentric, relying upon armchair speculation and a familiarity with neurosis, is partly derived from an unfortunate confusion with psychiatry. However, unlike the psychiatrist, the experimental psychologist is not primarily concerned with the abnormal. He works rather as a human biologist, attempting to establish the facts of human behaviour and to fit them into meaningful causal sequences, using ordinary scientific methods.

In the section on the evaluation of training it was suggested that one purpose in making measurements was to discover at what points a training programme might be improved. Obviously the instructor or training manager cannot continually experiment with his training methods—quite literally he has other things to do. This is precisely where the laboratory methods of experimental psychology can help. By "holding constant" all the extraneous influences which muddy one's understanding of a practical task it is often possible to arrive at generalizations about factors in training which have wide application. Generalizations or principles of this sort may show the trainer where to look. Given the appropriate information from the laboratory he will know what factors to look for and in which way they are likely to operate.

Obviously again it would be idle to pretend that such principles will provide automatic answers to practical problems. To employ them intelligently requires both imagination and insight. Generalizations will be of the form "other things being equal, the manipulative parts of an assembly task are more amenable to practice than are the place-to-place movements". Unfortunately it must be admitted that other things never are equal in real life situations. Nevertheless if we know in what way the other things are "unequal" we can piece our knowledge together to arrive at workable solutions to practical problems.

LIMITATIONS OF TRAINING

Although we are preoccupied by training, it will not do to forget that training is only one of several ways of getting greater efficiency. We train people because their skills do not match their tasks. However there are other ways of correcting a mismatch between men and their tasks. In order to arrive at the most effective man–machine combination, using "machine" in a sense wide enough to cover all the types of equipment and tools and apparatus which form part of modern life, we have three main alternatives.

First, we may pick out men who are already suitable for the job. This is the process of *selection*. Selection has been a traditional activity of industrial psychology, and may often be approached in a systematic way by the use of standardized tests. Again we may take persons who do not initially possess the necessary skills and alter their characteristics by *training*; this is our current concern. Finally we may reshape the task and the necessary equipment. This activity, which has come into prominence in recent years, is often called *human engineering*. It forms part of "applied experimental psychology" or of "ergonomics", which is defined as an inter-disciplinary approach to human problems of work, machine control and equipment design.

Studies of this last sort, in which the equipment for a task is evaluated by measurements of human performance on that equipment, have become of increasing importance since the last war. The work covers a wide range, from the detailed appraisal of features of dial design to the shaping of complex air defence systems involving large numbers of personnel. Once the possibility of "fitting the job to the worker" is considered it is clear that modifying the worker by training instead of modifying the equipment may be wasteful.

In a problem arising from defence research Siddall, Holding and Draper (1957) were faced with two alternative designs. In order to align a radio beam, with consequences which need not be described in detail, an operator might move a control for a given distance along a groove which constrained the *angle* of movement, or alternatively move it at a given angle within a circular rim which constrained the *extent* of the movement. An experiment showed clearly that the average operator was more accurate in adjusting the angle of his aim than the extent of his movement.

Often, as in this case, engineering considerations will permit two equivalent versions of an equipment, one of which is easier to operate than the other. When this happens it is pointless to use training techniques to overcome the initial disadvantage in time and errors which attaches to the more unsuitable version, unless of course large numbers of the unsuitable machines are already in service. The better answer is to modify the equipment. In our radar example then, the obvious solution was to select the version in which the operator made an angular adjustment, rather than to begin training on movements of different extent.

In some cases no amount of training will overcome the disadvantages of a task which has been designed without regard to human factors. This is true of the older techniques of submarine depth control for instance, where a diving control movement is followed by an appreciable delay before the results of the adjustment are apparent to the operator. Altering the electronic characteristics of the equipment in such a way that the operator has immediate knowledge of results will produce an improvement in performance which is apparently unequalled by training on the older version of the task (Taylor and Garvey, 1959).

In other cases we may make good the defects of an inefficient man–machine combination by training to the point where performance differences disappear. Unfortunately, as the evidence recently reviewed by Loveless (1962) shows, the effects of such training may not be permanent. Under the stress of concentrating on a rival task, carried out together with the learned task, performance may drop back to the old level; and it is probable that this happens too in the anxiety of an emergency. Such a "regression" is most likely to occur when the new training is designed to replace older, well-established habits by procedures which are incompatible with them; for instance in learning to turn a control clockwise instead of anti-clockwise.

Training is not the only means to better performance. Even in athletics new materials have changed the attainments, and perhaps the techniques, of pole-vaulting. Nevertheless, in many situations the equipment and the pattern of skill required by the task are near the optimum, or else are invariable for reasons of practical necessity. Artificial languages may be constructed in a way which takes account of human verbal predispositions, but real foreign languages exist and must be acquired. However efficient the design of a bicycle, we shall still need to acquire the skills of steering and maintaining equilibrium. The problems of efficient training therefore need attention, experiment and analysis.

TRAINING PROBLEMS

At this stage we should begin to consider in more detail what is involved in planning or reorganizing training. Training problems and the tasks to be learned vary in so many ways that it is not practicable to attempt any rigid classification. However we saw at the beginning of this chapter that the trainer has many different functions to perform, and it may help to group them under a few main headings.

Training devices. As we saw, the trainer may "provide the equipment". He will often take a hand in its design, or at least in its selection, since what he knows about training ought to determine the nature of the equipment. The way in which training devices are designed must depend crucially upon analysing the skill being trained, as must the training methods. Sometimes the equipment will be the machines used on the job, but often it will be a device for teaching a part of the final task, or a simplified version of the real thing.

Particularly when operating the real equipment is difficult or dangerous or costly the early stages of training will be undertaken on a "simulator"; that is, on a device which resembles the real equipment in its essentials, *from the point of view of the operator*. The Link trainer used for the teaching of flying skills is probably the best known example. What constitute the essentials must eventually be decided not by the degree of engineering precision in the simulator, but by the way in which the device affects training. If learning on the simulator is readily transferred to performance on the real task the device is successful; the criterion will be the amount of "transfer of training".

Motivation. The trainer will "encourage us to practise, and let us know whether we have improved or how we stand up to comparison with other people". The much-circulated but unpublished handbook on training by Miller (1953) lays great stress upon the part played by motivation in training and upon the role of the instructor in generating and maintaining motivation. It is easy to agree that the training process will be assisted if the learner wishes to perform the task and wishes to undertake the necessary practice, and if it is arranged that he is not discouraged by apparent failures.

A tempting slogan is "no learning without motivation", although it is not clear that this is strictly true. The scattered evidence we have on motivation presents rather a confused picture. For example Deese (1958) discusses cases of learning without motivation in animal experiments. Animals allowed to wander in a laboratory maze when not hungry still learn the way to food, but their learning is *latent*; that is to say one cannot tell from their performance that they have learned until motivation is introduced by making them hungry. Of course it is difficult to get such pure instances of learning without motivation in human skills, but one suspects that people's apparent performance is more affected by their degree of motivation than is their real learning.

Another snag is learning without awareness. It is possible to learn say, lists of words, without either meaning to learn or being aware of learning. In that case one can only introduce the idea of motivation by supposing that it is "unconscious". However, this line of argument really begs the question since the unconscious motivation is inferred merely because learning has taken place, while what we are querying is whether learning needs motivation. Motivation is really an unsatisfactory concept, and we can often leave it out of our thinking with some gain in clarity; it is simpler to say "giving children sweets makes them solve puzzles faster" than "giving children sweets increases their motivation, and with higher motivation they learn to solve puzzles faster". However, the term "motivation" is well-established and there are cases where its use seems adequately clear.

For example, too much motivation may make the learner over-anxious so that his performance is worse than it would have been at an intermediate level. It is a matter of common observation that people can sometimes try too hard. The amount which is "too much" seems to depend upon the difficulty of the task (Broadhurst, 1958); a simple task can take more motivation without deteriorating than a more difficult one. The factors of anxiety and confidence are intimately bound up with the effect of other factors in training and, especially in the early stages of learning, it may pay to take steps to reduce anxiety. One of the best reasons for training workers in quarters separate from the factory floor is the chance it offers them to become accustomed to new techniques and machinery in a situation where anxiety is easily replaced by confidence.

For practical purposes one may admit that some motivation is needed for efficient learning, even if only performance is affected directly by motivation. Most real tasks are learned by repeated practice, so that encouragement to perform well may be needed. People will not practise complicated tasks or attend to all the appropriate details if they are not motivated, and thus will not have the opportunity to acquire skill. Except in cases like schoolteaching, where pupils may be genuinely unwilling to learn, it is doubtful whether motivation needs separate consideration. To what extent any encouragement should be external, rather than stemming from the intrinsic efficiency of the training programme, is again not clear.

Extra motivation was added into a training scheme by Williams (1956), who encouraged groups learning to adjust electrical relays to compete with one another. This resulted in more work by the competing groups, but if anything the quality of work done by non-competitive groups was better, so that no real conclusions can be drawn to the effect that extra motivation is an asset. While the trainer should take steps to reduce anxiety where possible, it is probable that other motivational factors will be secondary to the proper design of the conditions which directly affect learning.

Training methods. It is no part of our present purpose to consider detailed recommendations for particular kinds of training. The methods used by the trainer will be good or bad to the extent that they are in agreement with the general principles governing human learning. These are examined throughout subsequent chapters by surveying the relevant research evidence, from which certain kinds of data have been arbitrarily excluded. For instance, techniques for developing strength and endurance like the systematic "circuit training" described by Adamson (1959) have been omitted, since these routines are designed primarily to effect physiological changes. A great deal of work on the analysis of skills has been excluded, in cases where the research does not bear directly on problems of training. However, it is not possible to proceed very far without considering the different kinds of skill for which training may be given and the basic attributes of skill learning.

TYPES OF TASK

There is a bewildering variety of human skills and activities, but we must be able to select out certain kinds of task from time to time on the basis of characteristics which they have in common. The nature of the task will determine our classification of the necessary skill and of the training appropriate for it. Just as we can classify cardboard boxes according to the way in which they vary along the dimensions of length, breadth and height, we can notice that tasks tend to vary in a few prominent ways. For instance, what we consider to be a single task may consist of one or more kinds of activity in a series.

Serial. When a job consists of doing several different things one after the other, in the right order, we tend to talk about *serial learning* in the laboratory and about *procedural training* as instructors. Many tasks consist of sequences and subsequences rather than of single movements or isolated activities. Starting a car for example will probably involve at least (a) ensuring that the gear lever is in neutral, (b) adjusting the choke, (c) switching on the ignition, and (d) pressing the starter button. The "gear lever in neutral" item may of course contain subsequences; if the car has been parked in gear (a) ascertain gear position, (b) depress clutch pedal, (c) adjust gear position, and (d) release clutch. This is a relatively simple procedure. The sequences involved in learning a poem, preparing a four-engined aircraft for take-off or in servicing an adding machine are far more protracted and complex.

Sometimes the trainee must learn both how to perform the individual items and how to carry out the correct sequence, although the component acts may be so simple that the emphasis in training

is on the order in which items are performed. Mistakes in the order
of activities are quite common in the early learning of unfamiliar
sequences. This is true of verbal tasks like learning by heart a series
of words or numbers and of bodily tasks like putting on a gramophone record or painting a floor.

Continuous adjustment. Tasks can be *continuous* as in steering a car,
where a series of adjustments flow one into the other, or else *discrete*
as in throwing a dart or hitting a billiard ball. An intermediate case
is represented by mounting a horse, which is a relatively short
segment of adjustive behaviour or perhaps a complex discrete act.
Tasks which vary along the discrete–continuous dimension tend to
vary in the amount of readjustment which is needed once the action
has started and in the span over which the learner must anticipate.
Planning or "programming" an action takes time—what is known
as the reaction time—and if the components of a skilled activity are
to follow one another in smooth succession he must learn to look
ahead. He must prepare for the next action while carrying out the
present one, learning to recognize in advance the important sights
and sounds which will determine his reactions. In a discrete task
decisions are made separately, with less overlap between one action
and the next.

Perceptual. Perception is the processing of information which
reaches our senses in the form of sights, smells, sounds, tastes, aches
and pains. These items of information are known as perceptual *cues*
or *stimuli*. The term *response* is often used to designate what we do
in response to these items of information. If a man is taught to
ring a bell or to say "crimson" whenever a red light is shone at him,
the red light is the stimulus and ringing the bell or saying "crimson"
is his response. His activities therefore have a *perceptual* element,
concerned with the relevant stimuli, and a *motor* element which
refers to the response. The term "motor" may include all the
muscular activities which produce different kinds of movement, but
when contrasted with the term "verbal" will often exclude those
movements of the larynx, palate, jaws, lips and tongue which give
rise to speech.

Different tasks vary in the stress which they place upon *perceptual*
information from the outside world or upon the elaboration of the
motor elements of the activity. Putting the shot and weightlifting are
largely motor tasks, while radar watchkeeping is almost entirely

perceptual, consisting mainly of analysing the visual data on the radar screen. Not a great deal is known about perceptual training, although there is work on *discrimination training*—teaching people to distinguish between closely similar objects; and on *identification training*—teaching people to recognize and name important objects, as in bird-watching or learning the parts of a sewing machine.

The distinction between largely perceptual and largely motor tasks seems to overlap another distinction which has been proposed. Knapp (1961) develops a suggestion with reference to sports that there is a continuum from "closed" skills, which are largely habitual, to "open" skills which are predominantly perceptual. Closed skills are illustrated by shot-putting while open skills are represented by fencing or football, in which the course of events is relatively unpredictable. The examples of fencing and football seem to fall half-way along the present perceptual–motor dimension, being less perceptual than keeping a radar watch, and probably also overlap the previous distinction between continuous and discrete tasks. Fencing and football also happen to have a social component, in that they involve predicting the behaviour of other persons, although this is incidental since playing against a robot might give rise to quite as complicated a task. There are many ways of classifying a complex field like that of skilled behaviour, but it is of little consequence what distinctions are made provided that the terms used have some descriptive value and, if possible, suggest feasible measurements.

SKILLED BEHAVIOUR

A person carrying out any skilled task needs three kinds of information. He needs information about what it is he is to achieve. This is the kind of information embodied in plans, instructions, objectives and standards. Next he needs information from the task itself, sensory information deriving from visual, tactual and similar changes in the equipment and the environment. Thirdly he needs information about the results of his own actions. He must not only make the right response at any part of the learned procedure but know that it is the right response.

The sequence of events is roughly as follows. Perceptual stimuli will reach the operator from all sides. As a result of his past experiences these stimuli will have meaning for him and may be treated as information. He will disregard the greater part of this sensory information, recognizing the important perceptual cues from the machinery or surroundings. The relevant stimuli are classified and processed by the brain, which then routes signals to the appropriate muscle groups. Muscles, joints and tendons have their own sense organs which provide what is known as *kinaesthetic* information, so that fresh perceptual information arises internally whenever a movement takes place. At the same time new information is created *externally* through the effects of muscular action upon objects which stimulate the other senses. He sees his hand turn a screwdriver, or hears his own speech. The next part of the activity is then guided by this fresh information, both kinaesthetic and external, as the cycle of events recommences.

A behavioural sequence is thus a complete loop consisting of input, output and *feedback*. Feedback is a useful term for describing the perceptual information which results from the operator's own activity. In this way a human or other living organism resembles the kinds of self-regulating devices often known as servo-mechanisms. A range of such devices from the simple thermostat to the automatic steering gear on the guided missile make use of the principle of feedback, and study of the way in which these devices operate has contributed a great deal to our understanding of sensorimotor skills.

Insight into the analogy between human behaviour and servo devices was achieved by Craik (1947); and Wiener (1949) has proposed that a single science called *cybernetics* should embrace the study of self-regulation in both biological and physical systems. For our purpose such a science needs to be supplemented by what we know about learning.

As we have seen, an organism makes use of two kinds of feedback, internal and external. The internal, kinaesthetic loop is vital to the performance of smoothly controlled actions. The patient with *tabes dorsalis*, in whom the kinaesthetic pathways are destroyed, moves jerkily and tends to overshoot when reaching for an object. To some extent he can compensate by using external, visual feedback, watching where he places his hands or feet, but this is a less efficient substitute. When he closes his eyes, of course, the only control he can exert lies in the accuracy with which he can pre-set his responses.

In normal persons, using the visual channel to regulate movements in this way is often said to be typical of the early stages of skill. It has been noted that a shift takes place with learning from the use of vision towards kinaesthetic control, and this has obvious advantages. Vision is then freed for the detection of advance cues so that time is saved and performance may be "streamlined". In old age, when skill deteriorates, there may again be a return from internal cues to a reliance on vision (Szafran, 1951).

There is, however, another way in which we may distinguish between internal and external feedback. Instead of considering the *channel* conveying the information we may look at the *source* of the information. For this purpose we may regard external feedback as referring to changes in the outside world and internal feedback as referring to changes in the organism. Notice that this does not quite correspond with the previous distinction. We have already seen for instance that external feedback—vision—may be used for the "internal" purpose of monitoring one's own movements. It is less often realized that the reverse may occur, the internal cues of kinaesthesis being referred to external sources.

Imagine for example that you suspend a large weight on the palm of someone's outstretched hand, his eyes being closed. For convenience we may also assume that his touch receptors have been anaesthetized. If now you release the string holding the weight, a great deal of rapidly changing kinaesthetic information will tell him unambiguously that something is happening *in the outside world*. In this sense then kinaesthesis may be used as a vehicle for external feedback.

It is to external feedback in this second sense that the term *knowledge of results* is most often and most naturally applied. The results in which we are interested for most training purposes are those which occur in the outside world, and knowledge of their occurrence may be conveyed to the operator through any of his sense organs. There is no uniformity of usage, however, and the reader should be warned that enthusiasts have occasionally extended the term to cover any kind of knowledge which the learner needs, whether or not this literally results from any of his actions.

2. KNOWLEDGE OF RESULTS

ONE of the most effective ways in which the trainer can influence the course of learning is by manipulating knowledge of results. A trainer can arrange to provide, or modify, or supplement the information which is fed back to the senses of the learner and which thereby determines his subsequent actions. The experimenter on the other hand may learn a great deal by depriving people of knowledge of results. Many experimenters have used this technique, with drastic effects upon learning.

REMOVING FEEDBACK

A straightforward demonstration of the need for knowledge of results was given by Thorndike (1927). He induced two groups of people—known as *subjects* in experimental work—to draw many hundreds of pencil lines of 3, 4, 5 or 6 inches over a period of several days, afterwards measuring the size of the errors which they made. One group drew lines while blindfolded and so deprived of visual knowledge of results. The lines drawn by this group were less accurate at the end of the experiment than they had been at the outset. For a second group, also blindfolded, Thorndike provided verbal knowledge of results by saying "right" or "wrong" after each line was drawn; a line was considered right if it finished within a quarter-inch target area. These subjects unlike the first group improved considerably, as one might expect.

A little later Trowbridge and Cason (1932) repeated this experiment, using several different kinds of knowledge of results. Their findings are shown in Fig. 2. Saying "right" or "wrong" improved people's performance, as it did with Thorndike, but telling them how much they were wrong by saying "plus two" or "minus seven" can be seen to give even greater accuracy. A fourth group of subjects gave rather a curious result which requires further examination.

In what is called a "well-controlled" experiment it is customary to use an extra group of subjects as a check when there is any ambiguity about what the experiment shows. In this case Trowbridge and Cason thought it might be objected that *any* form of words following the line-drawing response might be effective, whether or

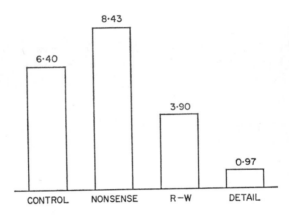

FIG. 2. The levels to which errors are reduced by different kinds of knowledge of results. The "control" group had no knowledge of results; the "nonsense" group were told nonsense syllables after each attempt; the "R–W" group were told merely whether they were right or wrong; the "detail" group were told exactly what their errors had been. After Trowbridge and Cason (1932).

not any information had been conveyed. To control for this possibility they therefore included a group to whom they spoke nonsense syllables like "gub" and "vop" after each line was drawn. As the diagram shows this group became clearly worse than the group which received no information whatever, so that we are in no doubt that it was necessary for knowledge of results to be informative.

However, this is not quite the whole story. Much later Seashore and Bavelas (1941) made a new analysis of Thorndike's experimental results. What they showed was that the group with no external feedback, although doing badly with respect to the accuracy of their lines, did become more consistent. They made large errors, but these were less variable. This too is a kind of learning, but a kind which we may assume to be due to kinaesthetic practice. Without external standards people will tend to match their previous attempts, while at the same time their perception of these attempts may become better developed.

In fact several lines of evidence lead us to believe that sheer familiarity with perceptual cues may enable us to distinguish better among them. This seems to occur when subjects have the opportunity to build up comparisons of auditory tones or fine visual cues. To some extent these inner comparisons afford the same kind of information as is given by comparing an attempt with an outside standard, although in most cases further knowledge of results will be needed to bring subjective judgments into line with reality.

ACTION AND LEARNING FEEDBACK

In order to understand knowledge of results better we must realize that it may function in more than one way. One may use the feedback which is present in any action situation to guide an *ongoing* response, or else to gain information which will enable us to improve the *next* response. Annett and Kay (1957) have brought out this distinction by comparing two possible methods of using a pair of kitchen scales. If one presses carefully on the pan while watching the pointer it is possible to reach an exact pressure, perhaps two pounds. Having once reached the two-pound mark in this way, however, there is no guarantee that one can repeat the same pressure with the pointer hidden. The feedback resulting from pressing the pan and watching the pointer has been used to guide immediate action.

On the other hand one might defer looking at the pointer until after making an attempt at the correct pressure. Seeing that the attempt is two ounces light one might press again a little harder, stop, and look at the pointer again, making repeated attempts which reach the two-pound mark by successive approximation. In this case, hiding the pointer for the next few attempts would cause us little difficulty, since we should have begun to learn the correct pressure.

The same kind of feedback information, the displacement of the pointer, may thus be used for two purposes. Miller (1953) has suggested that we distinguish these as *action feedback* and *learning*

B

feedback. Action feedback is not really knowledge of results—it is knowledge of the changing state of our attempts to produce results. It is learning feedback that the trainer hopes to achieve; that is, feedback which will leave behind it a changed ability to deal with similar situations. However, although the two functions of feedback are distinct, in practice we often cannot identify a perceptual signal as destined for action or learning. It may indeed serve both purposes. The operator may use it to adjust his current response, while remembering for future use the tendencies to error which his response revealed. Again, what is learning feedback for one operator, or in one situation, may be used as action feedback by another operator, or in another situation.

Part of the job of the trainer is to ensure that potential learning feedback is adequately used. There are in fact a number of stages in the process of modifying responses by learning, at each of which the trainer can attempt to help. Miller (1953) breaks the process down into ten stages, each of which may be further subdivided. It would be out of place to discuss these fully, but some idea of the complexity of the process should be indicated. Let us consider the case of learning to make a correct stroke in an arbitrarily simplified game of tennis.

(1) The feedback signal (the ball going out of court) must be discriminated. This involves knowing what to look for (the ball, the line demarcating the court), what constitutes an error (the point of contact outside the line), attending at the right moment (following the flight of the ball).

(2) The player must realize the connection between what he did (the original response; slicing the ball) and the resulting feedback (seeing the ball go out of court).

(3) He must connect what he did (the response) with what led up to it (the relevant stimuli; the feel of the racket, the ball coming towards him in a certain way).

(4) He must be able to produce a modified response (angling the racket in a different way) which could reduce the degree of error.

(5) He must associate the error signal with the relevant stimuli (remember the ball going out of court after approaching him in a certain way).

(6) He must realize that a new set of stimuli (the ball again coming towards him) are essentially similar to the previous stimuli.

(7) He must resist the tendency to produce the same stroke as before, and must substitute the modified response in its place.

We have now achieved a better response with the help of learning feedback. However, to prepare our learner for higher things the course of learning must continue.

(8) If the substitution of a better stroke is an effort, fortified by verbal mediation (muttering "don't slice it" or "watch the sideline"), he must keep practising until the correct response is automatic and the words drop out of the sequence.

(9) His practice must be carried out in a number of contexts, so that he will produce the right stroke against a different player, or in a high wind.

(10) If his new response tends to interfere with other necessary responses (remembering not to slice spoils his backhand) the interference must be reduced by further practice.

INFORMATION AND INCENTIVE

So far we have spoken only of the information value of knowledge of results. In fact it also appears to have a motivating function. Putting up day-by-day graphs of trainees' performance is a form of knowledge of results which may encourage them to better their efforts, or to compete with fellow trainees. Thorndike's technique of saying "right" or "wrong" gives subjects praise or blame as well as information; Thorndike himself regarded his experiment as a test of the effects of reward and punishment.

Several experimenters have noticed that people tend to lose interest in a task without knowledge of results. Elwell and Grindley (1938) used an apparatus in which subjects used two levers to direct a spot of light on to a target. Removing knowledge of results by switching off the light, so that subjects were unable to see where on the target they had landed, gave rise to the rather sudden drop in their scores shown in Fig. 3. All the subjects expressed displeasure and annoyance at the change in conditions, becoming bored and careless, and beginning to arrive late for experimental trials.

A later experiment by MacPherson, Dees and Grindley (1948) shows unexpected evidence of a motivational change when visual feedback is removed. Using the now familiar line-drawing task, they told subjects in advance that the next block of trials would be made without knowledge of results. Their scores dropped immediately, during the time that feedback was still available, an effect which can only have been motivational.

In one of the earliest experiments, by Arps (1917), the effect of knowledge of results was to prevent people's efforts from flagging. His subjects were required to lift weights repeatedly with one finger, which naturally soon fatigued. Allowing the subjects to see a con-

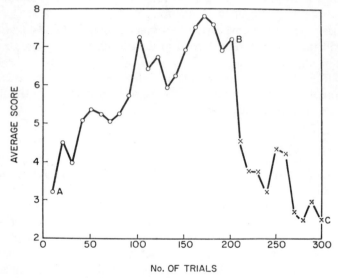

No. OF TRIALS

Fig. 3. The drop in performance with removal of knowledge of results. Learning takes place from point A to point B. At point B knowledge of results is removed. From Elwell and Grindley (1938).

tinuous graph of their efforts however maintained their performance extremely well. It is difficult to contend that this effect was due to the informational, rather than the incentive effect of knowledge of results, since no information was required beyond that already present in the task.

The fact that knowledge of results may have a motivational effect in "energizing" performance has led some psychologists to assume that it is basically similar to the rewards used in animal learning. Certainly trainers of human subjects may learn a great deal from the techniques of systemically selective reward developed by learning theorists. The foremost exponent of these techniques is Skinner

(1961); his methods, and their wider implications are well set out by Lundin (1961).

Skinner has shown how an animal such as a pigeon or a rat may be taught to perform any sequence of responses within its physical capacity. For example, a rat has been taught to mount a spiral staircase to a platform in its cage and then to push down and cross a raised drawbridge leading to another platform. It then climbs a ladder, draws over a cart by handling a chain, pedals through a tunnel then climbs a flight of stairs, squeezes itself through a tube, steps into a lift and raises the Columbia University flag. This starts the lift, which descends to ground-floor level where the rat presses a lever for a reward of food pellets. This chain of behaviour is built up by offering a reward, or something associated with a reward as soon as the animal responds in a way which is approximately suitable. Later only the more accurate responses are rewarded and the animal is led on to further stages in the sequence through a form of dumb procedural training, by a technique of successive approximation.

Such a description is reminiscent in many ways of the effects ascribed to knowledge of results, since we have already described the process of trial, error and feedback as one of successive approximation. The similarity appears greater if we consider, as do some learning theorists, that the rewards used in animal learning may be as valuable in informing as in rewarding. Possibly then both reward and knowledge of results have a dual function.

A CLASSIFICATION

We must next enquire what kinds of knowledge of results there are and how well they serve the purposes of incentive or information, and of action or learning feedback. There are a number of distinctions to be made. To make it easier to appreciate the classification which is proposed these distinctions have been set out in the form of a "family tree" in Fig. 4.

Knowledge of results may be *intrinsic* or *artificial*. In other words it may be present in the usual form of the task or else it may take the form of extra information added in for training purposes, like a buzzer which sounds all the time a rifle is on target. This second kind is often called "augmented" knowledge of results.

Artificial knowledge of results may be *concurrent* or *terminal*. This rather ugly piece of jargon is intended to convey the distinction between information which is present all the time a person is responding, as in watching a pointer while adjusting a control knob, and information which arises as a result of a completed response like the score of a dart throw. It will have occurred to many readers that intrinsic knowledge of results may also be concurrent or terminal. This is true. Similarly, most other distinctions shown in Fig. 4 may also be subdivided. The diagram only shows one set of branches for the sake of clarity.

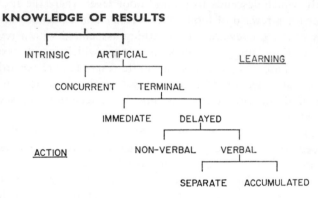

FIG. 4. Different kinds of knowledge of results.

Terminal, and concurrent, knowledge of results may be either *immediate* or *delayed*. These types in their turn may be *verbal* or *non-verbal*; that is to say they may take the form of words or scores, or else appear as physical indications like pointers or buzzers. Knowledge of results in a verbal form may be called knowledge of of score. This or its physical counterpart may be given after each response as *separate* knowledge, or else *accumulated* over several attempts and presented at the end of the series.

This classification is merely a convenience. Nevertheless, most practical examples can be adequately described in terms of these distinctions and, somewhat surprisingly, examples can be found to fit into most of the "spaces" it provides. For instance, accumulated, verbal, immediate, concurrent, artificial knowledge of results is given by a trainer shouting integrated error scores to a person trying to follow a moving target, although we shall avoid these concatenations of adjectives wherever possible. More importantly, it makes possible some generalizations concerning the functions of different kinds of knowledge of results. As shown in the diagram, the nearer an artificial item is to the left-hand side of the tree the more likely it is to function as action feedback; and of course the nearer it is to the right the more likely it is to be learning feedback. Furthermore there is probably a tendency for greater incentive value to follow the lines of learning feedback, although this is less clear.

INTRINSIC OR ARTIFICIAL

The difficulty about putting in artificial knowledge of results is that its effects may not last after its removal. Eventually the learner must come to rely upon the intrinsic cues. There is no point in learning to rely upon information which will not be there when training is finished. The success of techniques of augmenting feedback will depend upon whether they call attention to the intrinsic cues or make possible control of the relevant responses in a way which can later be taken over by the intrinsic cues. Of course intrinsic cues may contribute to the original learning, but by definition the trainer has no control over them. It is important here that he draws attention to them in various ways.

One problem which arises is that tasks exist in which the intrinsic feedback does not relate directly to the object of the activity. It may be clear *whether* we have achieved what we intended to do, but not whether *what* we intended to do was correct. If we are asked to give the Dutch equivalent for "stork", intrinsic auditory feedback will help us to approximate to the sound "ooievaar", but will not indicate whether we have used the right word. In such cases learning will not take place without knowledge of results, which must be injected artificially. More exactly, what the trainer must do is to provide *standards* against which we can assess our performance. It has already been pointed out that the learner must know what he is to do. Where this information is not available, it is essential to provide it. In this kind of situation the trainer is, in a sense, giving artificial knowledge of results indirectly by providing the standards which transform feedback into real knowledge of results.

Artificial feedback might be useful in training operators to appreciate cues of which they are not usually aware, as in the case of kinaesthetic sensitivity. Seymour (1954) discusses the handling of electrical pottery. Before firing, porcelain insulators must be held firmly as they are moved but not so firmly as to crush them. Seymour describes the use of dummy insulators with spring-loaded sides bearing on micro-switches; the right amount of finger pressure flashes on a white light, while pressing too hard switches on a red light. Operators then build up familiarity with the necessary pressures by transferring the dummy insulators rapidly from tray to tray, all the time attempting to keep the white light in view and to avoid even momentary flashes of the red light.

However, withdrawing artificial feedback may give disappointing results. Goldstein and Rittenhouse (1954) provide an example in training for air-to-air gunnery. Practice was carried out on a simulator, target aircraft being projected on to a curved screen in front of the gunsight assembly. With the "pedestal" sight which they used, pointing the gun in the right direction for azimuth and elevation presents less difficulty to trainees than the problem of ranging. Setting to the correct range, by the method of "framing", consists of squeezing a spring mechanism until a circle of dots just encloses the wing tips of the target aeroplane. The artificial feedback was a buzzer which sounded whenever the gun was on target. In similar work a filter which reddens the appearance of the aircraft has also been used for this purpose.

As Fig. 5 shows, the control group who worked without the buzzer made no real improvement after the first seven trials. A group getting buzzer information on 100 per cent of the trials appeared to improve, but show a drop on the fortieth trial when the buzzer was withheld. In a later experiment this drop continued until the sixtieth trial, at which stage no significant difference remained. In yet another experiment, when the trainees were transferred to a different kind of gunnery apparatus the buzzer group tended actually to perform worse than the control group.

The results of two other groups are also shown in Fig. 5. Both of these received buzzer information on 50 per cent of the trials, randomly chosen in one case and on alternate trials in the other. In each case the scores moved up and down depending upon whether or not the buzzer was used—this is what gives the "zigzag" appearance to the middle scores. The experimenters conclude that the effects of adding the buzzer were not permanent, and they do not recommend the use of this kind of artificial feedback. It is worth noting that the buzzer feedback is essentially of the concurrent type and will tend to behave as action feedback; the trainees tend to use it continuously to guide their responses rather than to evaluate their results.

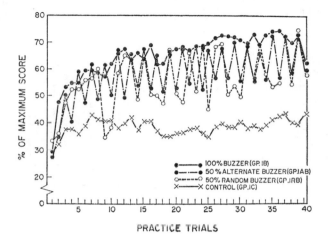

FIG. 5. Artificial knowledge of results. Performance in the two middle curves fluctuates as the buzzer is used or withheld. From Goldstein and Rittenhouse (1954).

CONCURRENT OR TERMINAL

At first sight the distinction between concurrent and terminal feedback may appear completely to determine whether action or learning is helped by a particular kind of information. The example of the kitchen scales which was used to illustrate the difference between the two functions contrasted the *concurrent* technique of watching the pointer moving with the *terminal* technique of making a reading when the push is complete.

However, there are many ways in which the operator can make later use of information which he gains during action feedback, so that it is unlikely that his performance will not improve at all. Also, the use he can make of terminal cues may be limited since, as we have seen, a number of psychological stages intervene between one

response and the next. There mere presence of terminal knowledge
of results will not by itself guarantee a fast rate of learning. It
remains true on the whole that, where the task is relatively simple,
we may expect the results of terminal feedback to be the more
permanent.

The comparison is clearly made in an experiment by Annett
(1959). His subjects practised pressing the handle of a plunger,

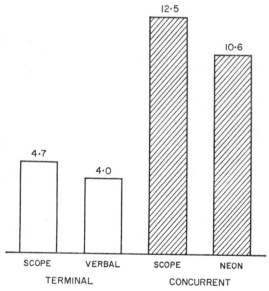

Fig. 6. Errors after learning with terminal or concurrent knowledge
of results. The effects of terminal knowledge of results are more
permanent, giving smaller errors on the "blind" trials. After
Annett (1959).

receiving artificial knowledge of results for the first thirty attempts.
The plunger was wired up to an oscilloscope so that concurrent
visual feedback, in the form of a moving light, resulted from pressing
the plunger. Roughly the same effect could also be produced
by a neon light which came on as the subject attained the target
pressure. Alternatively the experimenter could make the knowledge
of results take a terminal form by covering the oscilloscope face
until the subject had attempted to get the right amount of pressure.
The experimenter could then expose the oscilloscope, upon which
there was a printed scale, or else announce the error verbally.

What happened was that the subjects with concurrent feedback were able to reproduce the correct pressure with each response, while the terminal procedure gave fairly large errors at the outset which gradually reduced towards the end of the learning period. Next, the subjects were tested with no feedback. The subjects with terminal feedback did get worse, but only gradually. On the other hand, removing the concurrent feedback led to immediate and drastic loss of accuracy. After twenty "blind" trials responses became so wild that the apparatus was damaged several times. The average error scores for the first twenty test trials are represented in Fig. 6, which shows that the best condition of all was the verbal form of feedback.

One might imagine that giving concurrent feedback only intermittently would help to maintain performance. For instance, if a subject is given knowledge of results every other trial he can use the feedback during any trial as a kind of terminal knowledge of results at one remove from the previous "blind" trial. In another pressure-learning test Annett did compare intermittent with continuous knowledge of results. Despite the fact that knowledge of results on alternate trials only gives half the informed practice that continuous feedback offers, it did appear that there was an advantage in the intermittent procedure. However, the difference was not large and other studies of the same problem like the gunnery work of Goldstein and Rittenhouse (1954) have given negative results.

IMMEDIATE OR DELAYED

The effects of delay differ markedly between concurrent and terminal feedback. When the feedback is concurrent any delay or lag makes performance more difficult. With terminal knowledge of results the evidence suggests that mere delay is ineffective, or even conducive to learning, although it is true that the delay may offer an opportunity for interference from other sources.

Lag in concurrent feedback from continuous motor skills disrupts performance (Conklin, 1957). The longer a delay between moving a control and the corresponding movement of an indicator the worse performance becomes. In fact some deterioration occurs even if the delay is so slight that operators do not consciously notice it. The effects of this kind of lag are most dramatic in delayed feedback of speech (Lee, 1950). In these experiments a person speaks into the microphone of a tape recorder assembly, which stores his speech and replays it into his earphones about a quarter of a second later. The sound of his ordinary speech is masked off by the earphones and his effective feedback is the much louder delayed speech. In these circumstances the average person stutters, slurs his words or omits whole syllables, as if in a state of intoxication. Similar effects occur with delayed handwriting (van Bergeijk and David, 1959).

When the knowledge of results is terminal a rather different situation arises. The subject has merely to complete a response and attend to the relevant feedback in due course. It was originally thought that delay of knowledge of results was similar in its effects to the delay of reward with animal subjects, whose learning is adversely affected. An experiment by Greenspoon and Foreman (1957) did appear to show that increasing the delay up to thirty seconds caused decreasing learning, but many other studies of delayed terminal feedback have given negative or conflicting results.

One reason for the confusion is that several quite different time intervals are involved. We have seen that although the information arises as a result of a previous response it supplies learning feedback for the *next* response. It seems likely therefore that the delay before the next response will be at least as important as the delay before knowledge of results is given. The position is shown in Fig. 7. If the response (R1) which produces the knowledge of results (KR) is followed by the next response (R2) at a constant time interval, both kinds of delay are affected by a shift in the timing of knowledge of results. Changing from case A, with short delay of KR to the longer delay in case B has had the effect of reducing the delay before the second response, so that what is lost on the swings is gained on the roundabouts.

When we consider case C, where the interval between responses is longer, the implications are different. Both delays are long and we may expect some decrement in learning. Bilodeau and Bilodeau (1958a) have shown that this is true, and it is also true that, if anything, the delay *after* knowledge of results is more important than the delay beforehand. In order to find any substantial effects of delay they were led to investigate delays of as long as twenty-four hours or one week. Clearly, if the subject can make a response on one day and receive knowledge of the results of that response the following week, we may conclude that the mere passage of time is of little importance. Presumably what matters is whether or not the knowledge of results is unambiguously seen to belong to the appropriate response. In some cases we may even expect delay to be beneficial, forcing the learner to attend to the intrinsic cues.

On the other hand, if the feedback from the first response is withheld until *after the next response* as in case D of Fig. 7, the interpolated response may interfere so that learning will suffer. Lorge and Thorndike (1935) first showed this effect, using subjects

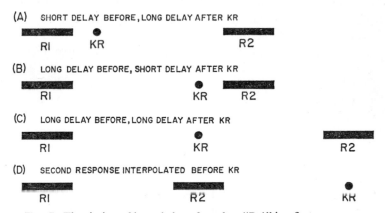

FIG. 7. The timing of knowledge of results. "R 1" is a first response; "KR" is the knowledge of results arising from R 1; "R 2" is a second response.

whose task was to throw balls over one shoulder at a target. In a simple lever-pressing task Bilodeau (1956) showed that the amount of learning depended upon the number of intervening responses— the more intervention, the less appeared to be learned.

Even so, we must be cautious in drawing conclusions. Again and again in considering the effects of knowledge of results it is easy to observe the effects on immediate performance or apparent learning, while forgetting that retaining the skill will depend upon the intrinsic cues when extra feedback is removed. Lavery and Suddon (1962) have recently shown the importance of tests of retention with reference to our present problem, the effects of delay with interpolated responses. Comparing delays of 0 and 5 responses, they showed that 30 training trials seemed to produce slower learning in the delayed group. However, after 90 trials the performance level was the same for both of the groups. What is more, removing knowledge of results left the delayed group *more skilled* than those trained with no delay. It may often be worth sacrificing speed of learning to ensure permanence.

VERBAL OR NON-VERBAL

Verbal knowledge of results tends to have lasting effects. However, it is difficult to find comparisions of verbal and non-verbal forms of information in which the other conditions have been equivalent, and it is possible that its advantages appear because it is usually terminal and often delayed.

For example, Karlin and Mortimer (1963) fed three kinds of artificial knowledge of results back to subjects carrying out a kind of tracking. In this task a target blip on an oscilloscope face moved backwards and forwards unless the operator corrected its position by turning a control knob, his aim being to keep the target stationary on an illuminated centre line. Verbal cues, or scores, were more effective both in training and on a subsequent test than were visual or auditory cues. A control group which received no supplementary cues performed worst.

Unfortunately, the verbal feedback consisted of time-on-target scores given after every trial and was thus terminal, while the auditory cue was the now familiar buzzer which sounded whenever the subject was approximately on target and was thus effectively concurrent. The visual cue was not feedback at all, but consisted of two extra lines delineating the target area which were present the whole time. We can therefore draw no firm conclusions from this experiment on the effects of verbal treatment. Annett's (1959) study discussed earlier shows a much clearer difference between terminal verbal and non-verbal knowledge of results, but the effect is rather small. It might be suspected in this case that the information presented on the oscilloscope was somewhat less easy to assimilate.

Some of the work by Goldstein and Rittenhouse (1954) in the experiments on gunnery training discussed earlier introduces yet another factor. The verbal knowledge of results which they compared with the buzzer treatment gave far more stable results. During training the level of scores for the groups with verbal feedback were lower, but did not fluctuate in the same way as those of the buzzer groups. After training, when all artificial feedback was removed the scores of the verbal group remained almost constant. However, it is important to notice that the verbal feedback, in addition to being terminal, carried far more information than did the buzzer. After each trial subjects were told what proportion of time they had remained on target, performance at different parts of each aircraft attack were compared and the current score was compared with the previous record. This is widely different from the buzzer treatment, and far more elaborate.

Clearly one of the advantages of the verbal method is the fact that it provides a convenient and flexible means for the trainer to convey a wide range of information to the subject. After any trial he may communicate a detailed analysis of responses and their effects, hints on form and stance, on what to look for in the task stimuli and information about standards of performance. In fact he may give a variety of types of information which shade into and out of knowledge of results. Also, basically factual feedback may be phrased in normative or emotive terms—"you're slipping; why not wait for the signal or have you got a train to catch?"—with resulting effects on motivation.

Of course, non-verbal methods may also be far more elaborate than appears in the buzzer example. Often the trainer will need detailed records of performance, which may be made available to the learner. Graphical methods for instance are often more efficient than verbal coaching when tricky movement sequences are to be taught. English (1942) showed that recruits may be taught to squeeze the trigger of a rifle by comparing recordings of each squeeze with those made by an expert. Quite clear and explicit verbal instructions were far less effective. Howell (1956) found similar results, using the force–time graphs of a runner's front foot movement to teach efficient sprint starts. It is obvious then that the kind of knowledge of performance which is given must depend upon analysis of the skill concerned, with insight into its points of difficulty.

The information given, whether verbal or non-verbal, may take many forms. The error or mismatch between the result of an action and its target may be transformed in many ways. It may be magnified or distorted, or a constant may be added (Bilodeau and Bilodeau, 1961) and behaviour will usually be regulated accordingly, although the effects may be transient. Denny and others (1960) successfully used a verbal scale consisting of imaginary units called "glubs"; such a scale has an internal consistency which averts the disruptive consequences of the nonsense syllables mentioned earlier. The fact that such information may be imprecise seems not to matter greatly.

Precision, like delay, is a factor which experiments show to be less important than one might expect. For example, varying the size of the target seen by the subject while scoring him to closer limits makes very little difference (Green, 1955). What matters most is the relation between the precision of any artificial feedback and the intrinsic or internal feedback. Over-precise artificial feedback may act as a "crutch" during training, again with the danger that performance sags after its withdrawal, as in an experiment on the accuracy of line-drawing by Holding and Macrae (1964).

Of course, there are cases in which the basic task contains very few or not any intrinsic cues. Trying to make judgments of the amount of time which has passed is an example (Waters, 1933). In this kind of work, where the subject has little else to go on, the efficiency of learning seems to vary directly with the accuracy of the knowledge of results.

SEPARATE OR ACCUMULATED

On the evidence so far available it is not easy to decide what is the best length of performance upon which to report, but several kinds of information may all be available. The accumulation factor may vary from piecemeal movement-by-movement correction to the vastly condensed knowledge of results afforded by a degree examination after several years of study.

The effects of more accumulated knowledge of results may be lasting and appear to have incentive value, but if accumulated over too long a period the effect on performance is so slight that its permanence has no attraction. A tracking study by Smode (1958) suggests that training with separated feedback is superior to accumulated verbal feedback, but the separated form contains both visual and auditory elements so the conclusion is not clear cut. Separate or item-by-item correction is very effective in teaching machines (Chapter 8) or in the learning of Morse code (Keller, 1943).

There is no doubt too that accumulated knowledge of results can be extremely valuable. An elaborate experiment on accumulated verbal feedback was carried out by Alexander, Kepner and Tregoe (1962). This study attempted to modify the learning of groups rather than individuals, by giving information to air defence radar crews at "debriefing" exercises held after training exercises. The job of each crew of thirteen men was to detect and follow the movements of any aircraft in their operational area, to report hostile aircraft to adjacent radar sites and to control tactical action by interceptor pilots where necessary.

During training a number of exercises were held, providing data on the efficiency with which each crew detected and kept contact with the aircraft they were to track. This information was discussed at extensive debriefing meetings with some of the crews at the end of each exercise, the crews being encouraged to identify problems arising in the exercise and to work out revisions of their operational methods. After training, crews were tested on a "unique problem" offering relatively stressful situations which had not previously been encountered. The proportion of aircraft tracks during certain critical flights which were established and maintained by the crews who had debriefing throughout training are compared in Fig. 8 with the performance of two uninformed control crews. Debriefing gave results twice as good as the control figures.

Fortunately there is usually no reason why separate and accumulated results should not both be given. The combination of separate, response-by-response information with periodic progress reports or knowledge of score is unexceptionable. Knowledge of progress is usually a kind of "second-order" knowledge of results. That is to say it consists of relating the accumulated knowledge of results of many individual actions to some kind of composite goal and is thus knowledge of results, of results. Care is needed in setting up the goals against which progress is matched since these will determine the success or failure experienced by the learner.

Failure affects a measure called the "level of aspiration", which has little to do with aspirations but indicates how well the learner thinks he will do on his next attempt. At present, studies of this kind of estimate seem to provide little of interest with reference to permanent learning, although it is easy to show disturbances of performance as a result of failure. An example is provided by

Willingham (1958), who examined the records of 2500 flying trainees. After failures on a check flight, these students, particularly the better ones, obtained lower training marks for one or two days. However, little effect remained only four days later.

The effects of failure are complex, and the relation of failure to learning is indirect. Nevertheless it does seem desirable on common-sense grounds to make knowledge of progress as favourable as

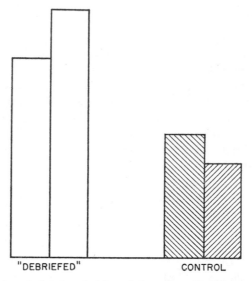

FIG. 8. Accumulated verbal knowledge of results. The percentages of "tracks" established and maintained by radar crews with and without "debriefing". After Alexander, Kepner and Tregoe (1962).

possible, an effect which can be arranged by manipulating the target set for the learner. One way of keeping failure to the minimum is to set him to better his own previous performance, rather than to reach an arbitrary standard. Like other training procedures, such techniques should be evaluated in actual practice.

SUMMARY

We have seen that active behaviour is constantly regulated by the feedback of information conveying knowledge of the results of his actions to the learner. Some kinds of feedback are *intrinsic* to the task to be performed, while the task may also be augmented by *artificial* feedback. Sometimes the task itself is artificial, in which case no progress will be made unless the trainer provides *standards* against which performance may be seen to be right or wrong. It will always pay the trainer to draw attention to the intrinsic cues and to the use which can be made of them, but the value of artificial kinds of knowledge of results needs more examination.

Terminal. It is important to distinguish between changes in immediate *action* and performance and changes which give rise to more permanent *learning*, since quite dramatic manipulations of action feedback may have only temporary effects. The terminal knowledge of results coming after an action is more likely to assist in learning than is concurrent feedback, whose function is rather to regulate the actions during which it occurs. Giving concurrent feedback only intermittently is of possible assistance.

Delayed. Lags in action feedback are disruptive, but learning is relatively unaffected by the delay of terminal knowledge of results. The time interval between feedback information and the next response is of some importance, but the major factor is the total interval between responses. Interpolating other responses between knowledge of results and the action from which it stemmed seems inadvisable, although at least in simple tasks the effects may again be temporary.

Verbal. Knowledge of *score* is likely to help the learner, although the design of experiments using verbal feedback has often been unsuited to direct comparisons with non-verbal equivalents. Verbal knowledge of results can convey a variety of types of information and persuasion. Points of technique which are obscure to the learner may be made clear by non-verbal methods.

Accumulated. Separate knowledge of results gives the learner the information he needs for step-by-step correction of his actions. Knowledge of *progress* is gained by relating accumulated knowledge of results to long-term goals. Particularly when linked to analysis and discussion, accumulated knowledge of results is likely to improve training. Changing the long-term goals of the learner will affect his experience of success and failure.

3. GUIDANCE

WE HAVE seen that the purpose of providing knowledge of results is to enable the learner to modify his actions. In this way his responses become successively more accurate, and the effects which he produces gradually align themselves with the standard he has been set. This is the familiar course of learning under the conditions of trial and error. So familiar, in fact, is the idea of trial-and-error learning that we may easily forget that the amount of error committed is often under the control of the trainer. It is interesting to ask whether training is improved when the actions of the learner are circumscribed in various ways, so that the errors he may make are reduced, or entirely prevented.

RESTRICTING ALTERNATIVES

For instance, if subjects are to be taught the definitions of psychological terms, we may print a number of alternative answers. One will be correct in each case, and the others wrong. If we get the subject to punch the answer which he thinks is right, we can provide immediate knowledge of results by arranging a series of holes in a board behind the answer sheet. Punching the right answer will give positive knowledge of results, since the punch will enter a backing hole, puncturing the paper; punching a wrong answer will give negative knowledge of results, as the punch merely jars on the backing. A device of this sort is a "teaching machine", with which we shall be concerned in a later chapter.

Using this kind of punchboard, Kaess and Zeaman (1960) manipulated the number of errors made, by varying the number of alternative answers. There were thirty different questions. One group tried working through the set, choosing between five alternative answers. If their first choice was wrong, they were allowed to try again until they hit the right one. Another group had four choices, another three, and another two; while the group of greatest interest had only one answer available, the correct one. A further group, shown as 5NC on the graph, had five choices with no knowledge of results—there were no holes through which to punch. Once the groups had worked through the set of questions, they were given further trials; this time, all the groups worked with five alternatives.

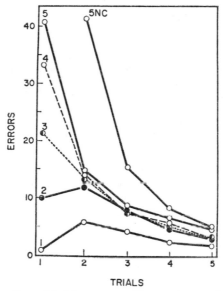

TRIALS

FIG. 9. The effect of limiting errors. The numbers at the beginning of each curve show the choices available to learners during the first trial. Group "5NC" had no knowledge of results. From Kaess and Zeaman, 1960.

In Fig. 9 we are shown the learning curves of these different groups. Two things are quite clear. The "5NC" group, with no knowledge of results in the first trial, are at a disadvantage against the remaining groups. Further, the group with only one alternative performs far better than those with more. This group is effectively forced to make a correct response to each question.

Further analysis of their results suggests that people may come *to learn the errors which they commit*, and tend to repeat them. Later, these erroneous responses will have to be "unlearned". A similar problem arises in motor learning. Kay (1951) has demonstrated that this difficulty exists in a serial task, where morse keys were used to extinguish pilot lights to which they were arbitrarily connected; older subjects in particular find it hard to change errors which they make early in training. Obviously, if we can find ways of controlling the responses made by the subject, we can ensure that what he learns to do is never wrong.

TYPES OF GUIDANCE

There are many methods for minimizing errors in early learning, and experiments have been carried out in an attempt to see how effective these techniques are. "Guidance" is the description traditionally assigned to these methods. The term is not particularly explicit, and we must make some further distinctions before surveying the results.

Physical restriction. To prevent overt errors from appearing, we can often "block off" incorrect movements, by making them physically impossible. A harness for controlling a golfer's swing makes use of this principle for instance. In this kind of guidance, the learner provides the power, while the direction or extent of the movement is externally controlled. Sometimes, physical restriction may take the form of providing support for part of an activity, so that the remainder may be practised freely. The use of floats and belts in swimming practice is an example of this partial guidance.

Forced-response. Another method, the most direct, is to control a pattern of movement by actively transporting the limb or the whole body of the subject; it appears, for instance, that the Balinese use this method in passing on the movements of their dance gestures and other ritual activities (Bateson and Mead, 1942). Dual control devices may take this form, although these are usually employed more for reasons of safety than of training. The forced-response learner does not actively initiate his responses, but remains overtly passive. In the early experimental work, the guidance was usually given by hand, although nowadays a number of mechanical methods have been developed.

Visual guidance. As we have seen, most skills are controlled in the early stages by external cues, predominantly visual cues. Often, visual materials may be laid out in such a way as to show the learner what to do at each point. The plan view of a maze, which is eventually to be traced blindfold, may be laid out before the learner to give him preliminary visual guidance; he may either trace through using the plan, or store the visual information for later use, taking no immediate action.

Verbal guidance. The giving of verbal instructions is another way of making sure that the learner does not have to use trial-and-error methods. As Annett (1959) has pointed out, we may often regard guidance techniques as giving "knowledge before" a response, rather than "knowledge after" in the form of feedback. Not all verbal methods can be considered guidance techniques, of course, and the use of words in training raises a number of other issues which are best dealt with in a later chapter.

ANIMAL WORK

The problem of guidance was first raised by Thorndike (1898), working with cats. Such animal work throws light on many issues in the problems of guidance with human subjects. Thorndike used a "forced-response" technique, in which cats were lifted and dropped through a hole in the top of a puzzle box. Escaping from the box by pulling a loop brought them a reward of fish. These animals failed to learn to re-enter the box of their own accord, even when lifted and placed next to the hole; on the other hand, animals which were made to go through the door at the front learned readily to repeat the performance.

The Thorndike experiment has been interpreted as adverse to guidance; yet the second group were also guided. In any case, both Cole (1907) with raccoons, and Hunter (1912) with white rats, found guidance effective in similar situations. Cole's results are particularly impressive. All his raccoons ran back inside boxes into which they had been lifted, by way of the hole in the top if the door was closed; they would also take short cuts when possible. They learned to undo fastenings by being "put through" manually. Further, if the experimenter guided the unfastening with one paw, the skill could be transferred to the other paw, or to the nose, if this were required. For nine of the eleven puzzle boxes, the time taken to learn by guidance was about half the time by trial-and-error. Finally, animals unable to learn difficult problems unaided managed to perform successfully after guidance.

Finding the way through a maze is a convenient task for experiments on serial learning, since it is easy to record the errors made in wrong turnings and the difficulty of the task is easily changed by adding or taking away pathways. The maze was first used in experimental psychology by Small (1900), who constructed a model of the Hampton Court maze for use with laboratory rats (Fig. 10). Mazes of different patterns have been used in a wide variety of early experiments. A common technique for guidance in such mazes is to close off the incorrect pathways, or alleys, by doors which may be removed after training. In this way, several early investigators examined the effects of differing amounts of guidance, and of

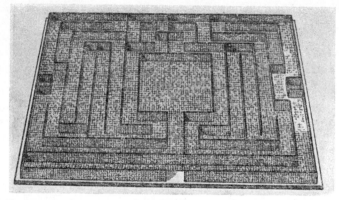

Fig. 10. Small's model of the Hampton Court maze. From Munn (1950).

introducing or withdrawing guidance at different stages in the learning process. Koch (1923), for instance, showed that one such trial of restrictive guidance was usually as effective as having the rat run unaided through the maze several times. Tsai (1931) tried withdrawing the guidance gradually, alley by alley, but the effects were unsatisfactory.

Another technique was that of Alonzo (1926), who attached leads and collars to his rats, guiding them through a maze with indifferent success. Gleitman (1955), and McNamara, Long and Wike (1956), have more recently achieved learning with a form of visual guidance, by the device of pulling their rats through a maze on a trolley.

Quite a different question was raised by N. R. F. Maier's use of manual guidance, in a series of studies on the effects of frustration which have obvious relevance to problems of human neurosis. In these experiments, rats were trained to jump from a stand at one of two doors; one door might be distinguished by a black circle on a white card, the other bearing a white circle on black. For each jump, one door could open to admit the rat to a food reward, the other being fixed. A rat choosing to jump at the fixed door bumped his nose, and fell to the safety net below. If necessary, rats were prompted to jump by a blast from a compressed air nozzle.

Two kinds of problem could be posed. In the easier version the reward door was always on the right, or on the left, so that a *position* response was required; in the more difficult case the rewarded door changed from side to side in an irregular way, but was always marked by the same pattern card, so that a *discrimination* response was required. Both of these problems could be made insoluble, by rewarding the rats only on a chance basis. Under the frustration of this procedure, they tended to develop fixations, jumping time after time to the same card or position in a way that was impossible to correct by hundreds of ordinary trials. It was soon found, however, that restrictive guidance could break such fixations, by manually preventing a fixated rat from jumping to the wrong door.

Maier and Klee (1945) explicitly compared guidance with trial-and-error methods in this situation. Training on soluble and insoluble problems produced twenty-six rats with position fixations, and thirty with ordinary, flexible, learned position habits. Both groups were then required to learn a discrimination response instead; half by trial-and-error, and half after guidance for the first thirty trials. In both groups, far more learned the new discrimination after guidance, and far fewer developed fixations (Table 1). Further analysis of these results suggests that the advantage of this kind of guidance lies more in teaching them to abandon the former position habit than in helping to form the new discrimination.

TABLE 1

Number of animals given discrimination training

	Satisfactory learning	Forming fixations
After guidance	21	3
Without guidance	9	19

Later, Maier and Ellen (1952) attempted to discover whether the effects of early guidance persisted into the solution of other problems. After guidance for the last ten of every fifty trials in a discrimination problem, 90 per cent of the guided rats achieved a solution, against 64 per cent of the unguided group. On the next problem, an insoluble one, both groups persisted equally with the previous solution. However, when a soluble problem was offered—different from the first one—36 per cent of the unguided rats developed fixations, compared with only 6 per cent of those who were initially guided. It appears, then, that early guidance may help to preserve flexibility in the face of frustrating conditions.

HUMAN MAZE LEARNING

Like laboratory animals, human subjects may be asked to learn model mazes, usually by attempting to trace through the correct path with a finger or stylus. Koch (1923), who guided rats by blocking off blind alleys, used a similar technique in teaching human subjects the same maze pattern.

The effects of guidance were in general far poorer with human subjects. It is not necessary to assume that rats are better able to profit from training than human subjects, since there are several differences in the experimental method which appear sufficient to account for the discrepancy. First, there is the matter of maze size. The rats performed in a maze approximately four feet square, and the mechanics of getting through it gave no difficulty. The human version was less than six inches square, and constituted quite a delicate manipulative task. Koch admits that subjects might spend several minutes working the stylus back and forth attempting to follow *the true path*, so that it is hardly surprising to find that hints on blind alleys fell upon somewhat preoccupied fingers. Again, human mazes are run "blindfold", in that the maze is screened off by a black curtain. Thus, we may expect broad differences in the learning of the maze; and the fact is that while unguided humans needed an average forty-four trials to learn the maze, the rats required only thirty-four.

What is more, the rats had an advantage in the guided runs which was completely lacking in the human experiment. In the rat maze, blocking off the blind alleys was achieved with doors of glass thus giving them not only knowledge of the correct response, but juxtaposing and distinguishing this from what was incorrect, since they could see down each blind alley. This is an important factor in other kinds of guidance. Finally, the human learners were guided by stealth. The experimenter merely slipped the blocks quietly in, or removed them without warning. This procedure seems as likely to disrupt learning as to assist it.

Even so, two guided trials at the outset helped people to learn in seven less trials than a free learning group. Thereafter, increasing the number of guided trials tended to bring rather less improvement, or sometimes deterioration; although one's evaluation of this effect will depend upon how the information on trials and errors is used, and upon whether the guided trials are included in the comparison. Carr's (1930) conclusion on the decrease of efficiency with larger amounts of guidance, which has been widely quoted, is based on a kind of index. He divided the saving in trials by the number of guided trials, to arrive at a measure of the effectiveness per guided trial. However, this figure must go down as the number of trials increases. If two initial guided trials are each worth four ordinary trials, then twenty guided trials would only appear equally effective if they saved eighty of normal practice. This is almost double the forty-four taken by the control group; and clearly one cannot save non-existent trials.

Error scores present a somewhat similar difficulty. As learning proceeds, fewer errors are made, and it is not reasonable to expect guided trials to achieve as great a saving as in the early stages. Incidentally, the error scores do not always present quite the same picture as the number of saved trials. Some groups make less errors over more trials, for instance, which further complicates interpretation. Further, errors in maze learning may take the form of retracing parts of the true path, as well as entering blind alleys; and guidance may affect the two kinds of error unequally.

Despite these complexities, we may gain some idea of the course of events from considering merely the number of trials saved in learning the maze, as the amount and position of guidance varies. The "position" of guidance refers to Koch's introduction of different numbers of guided trials at various stages in the first third of the learning process. These relationships are laid out in Fig. 11; the pattern is roughly similar if the guided trials are included in the total number of trials needed, although naturally the values are lower. What seems to happen is that the value of guidance falls after the first few trials, and then rises again. It is possible to discern a similar pattern in most of the error scores.

The explanation probably lies in the method of guidance employed. Inserting blocks in the blind alleys effectively changes the maze pattern, and the learner's task. A few early trials will help him to locate the goal, and to build up a rough internal map of the true path. Changing the pattern during the critical period soon after the

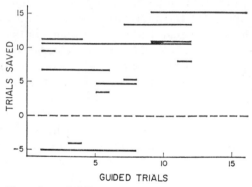

FIG. 11. The value of different amounts of guidance. The number of ordinary trials saved seems less when guidance is introduced or taken away shortly after learning has begun. After Koch (1923).

start of learning will tend to upset this process, although there will be less disruption by the time the learning is well advanced. Thus we shall expect to find that introducing a basic change soon after the initial trials, either by beginning or by ending guidance, will tend to hold back learning.

MAZES AND FORCED-RESPONSE

A different prediction will hold for forced-response methods, where the subject is forewarned that guidance is being given. Ludgate (1924) tried out two maze patterns, "carrying" subjects through the maze by grasping the stylus just below the learner's hand. In general, this kind of guidance seemed more effective than the restriction form, and was much more effective than unguided learning, particularly with the more difficult maze. At its best, eight initial trials of guidance saved twenty-one ordinary trials. Introducing guidance at different stages of learning gave the reverse effect to that of Koch, in that the number of trials saved tended to rise after the first few trials, and then to decline. For example, if four guided trials were to be given, they seemed to produce most saving if they began on the fifth learning trial. With this kind of guidance, the task is not disrupted by the change in pattern which affected the blocking method; and we may assume that a few initial trials allowed subjects to "get the hang of" the task, and to make the best use of guidance when it appeared.

Ludgate also examined transfer of training. Those persons who had been trained on one of the mazes next learned the other, and their scores were compared with the original control groups. Surprisingly, the group who had been given guidance on the first maze all transferred their learning more readily to the second. The amount of transfer tended to increase in proportion to the number of errors saved on the first maze; and, for the more difficult maze, in proportion to the amount of guidance which had been given.

As we have implied, it is difficult to decide whether guided trials should be counted in the learning scores, or treated as a kind of extra, like verbal instructions. The difference made by including or excluding the guided trials is brought out clearly in Waters' (1930) work on relatively massive amounts of guidance (Fig. 12). The smallest amount here, twenty trials, is greater than the largest amount used in the previous studies.

One of the arguments for excluding guided trials is that they each take far less time, and cover far less distance in the maze, than the corresponding control trials, so that guided subjects have less total experience of the maze. By pairing each guided subject with a control subject, and giving each man guided runs for the length of time taken by his unguided opposite number on the first trial, Waters and Ellis (1931) attempted to equate the time spent in training. The guided group tended to perform better, although the effect was not clear-cut in the scores of those who completed the task. Almost twice the proportion of unguided subjects failed to learn the maze in the number of trials allowed.

Waters (1931) also tried incorrect guidance, artificially imitating the path taken by unguided subjects. This reduced the number of

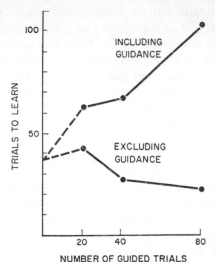

FIG. 12. Including or excluding guided trials from the number of trials needed to learn a maze. After Waters (1930).

trials required but, as one might expect, tended to increase the number of errors made during learning.

ADJUSTIVE SKILLS

The learning of mazes is essentially a procedural skill, depending more upon the retention of sequential, spatial information than upon fine sensori-motor control. We have examined the maze-learning work at some length, since much of our knowledge about the effects of guidance is derived from these sources. The questions raised by guidance in adjustive skills have received rather less attention.

The kind of operation which calls for continuous, adjustive movements is typified by the "tracking task". Driving a car, turning a cube on the lathe, or catching a ball, all require some kind of moment-to-moment adjustment of responses to a target. If the target is stationary, and the operator's responses are directed towards correcting deviations from the target, the task is *compensatory*. If the target is changing, and the operator is required to locate and keep pace with the target, his task is one of *pursuit tracking.* Steering a car on a steady course down a straight road requires compensatory tracking; steering it round a bend involves pursuit tracking. Other things being equal, pursuit tracking tends to be the easier (Poulton, 1952). No data are available on guidance in compensatory tracking. Such guidance would consist only of control movements, giving only kinaesthetic information. This occurs because the indicators in a self-tracked compensatory task would remain stationary, so that no visual cues would be available.

An evaluation of forced-response guidance in pursuit tracking was attempted by Holding (1959). Two different target courses were used, generated by a cam which moved the pointer up and down a vertical scale. Under normal conditions the subject used a large control knob to follow the target movement with a second pointer. For guidance runs, the motion of the target course cam was geared directly to the control knob and the two pointers, so that subjects merely gripped the knob lightly while the apparatus tracked itself. Only short amounts of guidance were given, as the learning curve flattened out very quickly and it would have been difficult to evaluate large amounts. The effect of two minutes' guided tracking was to reduce the error scores to the same level as normal practice produced in the same time. This learning was not specific to the target course for which guidance was given, because transferring guided and unguided subjects to the other course resulted in equivalent amounts of saving.

The next step was to split the guidance into separate components. Full guidance, of the kind described above, was compared with visual guidance and kinaesthetic guidance. The kinaesthetic training group were blindfolded while feeling the rotation of the control knob, and the visual group folded their arms while watching the pointers tracking in unison. The contribution to learning due to visual guidance was about 60 per cent of the error saved by full guidance, while kinaesthetic guidance seemed to account for only 20 per cent. Melcher's (1934) results on children's maze-learning, while incomplete, seem to parallel these findings. Possibly these proportions would have differed, had guidance been given after some preliminary practice. Kinaesthetic maze guidance appeared better after some exposure to the task, in the experiment by Ludgate (1924); and in the tracking case it may give information before the subject is ready to make use of it, while visual guidance permits the learner to see at the outset what is required.

Guidance in turning a handwheel at a constant rate was compared with knowledge of results by Lincoln (1956). During learning, three methods were used. The handwheel might be turned by a motor at the standard speed of 100 revolutions per minute; it might be turned at a rate corresponding to the error on the subject's previous trial, and the subject told whether this represented a negative or a positive error; finally, the previous error might be given verbally. Although the verbal method appeared slightly better during training, when performance was measured later without any supplementary cues, the accuracy of the three groups was about the same.

The other form of guidance—the restriction method—was tried out in two-handed tracking of a clover leaf pattern (Bilodeau and Bilodeau, 1958). Subjects could either track along a flush surface or along a recessed path which restricted their movements. Transferring from restrictive guidance to free tracking saved about one day's practice, as did transferring from free movement to the guided version of the task. Clearly, restriction training has some value in continuous adjustive skills, although no direct comparison with forced-response methods is available.

GRADED MOVEMENTS

Further evidence on the results of physical manipulation of human responses comes from work on single adjustive movements. Holding and Macrae (1964) adapted the line-drawing experiment to permit the comparison of forced-response and physical restriction with two kinds of knowledge of results. Six groups of subjects were blindfolded and instructed to move a knob along a rod for a distance of exactly four inches. After a set of twenty attempts, nine sets of training trials were given by different methods, followed by a test set of a further twenty trials. Learning was measured in terms of the difference in error score between the first and final test sets.

A control group received no guidance or feedback throughout the experiment. Another group received guidance in all the training trials, from a modified door-spring which towed the hand along, decelerating to a stop at four inches in a manner resembling an ordinary human movement. The problem of accurate simulation in guided movements is probably important, but has hardly received experimental attention. A third group received "distributed guidance"; that is to say, guidance was alternated with normal practice for successive sets of training trials. For the fourth group, restrictive guidance was provided by a stop screwed into the rod at the four-inch mark. The training method for a further group was "right–wrong" knowledge of results, the last group receiving detailed knowledge of results in terms of the amount and direction of error.

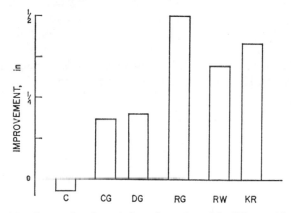

Fig. 13. Comparing knowledge of results with different kinds of guidance. Each bar shows the amount learned during training. "C" was a control group; "CG" learners had forced-response guidance throughout; "DG" was forced-response on alternate trials; "RG" was guidance by restriction; "RW" was "right-wrong" information. "KR" was full knowledge of results; After Holding and Macrae (1964).

Figure 13 shows the results obtained. The two kinds of forced-response training had some effect, but restriction gave a greater gain, and was quite as effective as knowledge of results. The superiority of restriction was unexpected, although the activity it allows to the subject may be beneficial, and hitting the stop may have some emphasis value which the forced deceleration lacked. Again, just as restrictive guidance materially altered the maze-learning task for the subject, so forced-response guidance alters the character of discrete movements. If anything, the learner is pulling against the door-spring, a movement opposed to the push required in the test trial. Thus, while the movements required in training and testing are

c

identical for restriction, they are antagonistic in the forced-response case. Of course, this is only true when the task is to push; in a pulling, or releasing, task we might expect the advantage to be reversed.

This last prediction has been tested with a further modification of the previous apparatus (Macrae and Holding, in press). Figure 14 shows the results of two groups repeating the restriction and guidance conditions of the first experiment, compared with the results of these training methods on a releasing task. The new test conditions resembled the "deadman's hand" mechanism of the tube train; the control knob was pulled along at a constant speed when gripped by the subject, and stopped when he released it at his estimate of four inches. For this new task, forced-response training appeared to be superior to restriction, as predicted.

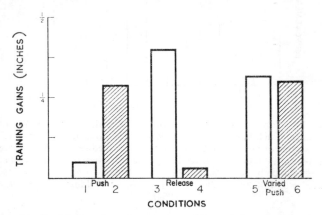

Fig. 14. Restriction, forced-response and knowledge of alternatives. 1. Forced-response (push task). 2. Restriction (push task). 3. Forced-response (release task). 4. Restriction (release task). 5. Varied forced-response (push task). 6. Varied restriction (push task). Plain bars are forced-response, hatched bars represent restriction.

At the same time, a further idea was tested. Guided subjects, while prevented from learning errors, are usually deprived of the chance to build up a range of experience by making a wide selection of responses. However, guidance is a flexible technique, and it is equally possible to give guided experience of a range of responses. Two further groups were therefore given guidance and restriction at 2, 3, 4, 5 and 6 inches, before testing on the four-inch pushing task; these results also appear in Fig. 14. Forced-response appears to be improved, although the restriction group does not. It seems likely that this multiple restriction technique, together with simple restriction and knowledge of results in the previous experiment, have encountered a limit on learning. It is difficult to better the final error scores, and wider differences between experimental conditions might only appear with fewer training trials.

KNOWLEDGE OF ALTERNATIVES

These multiple guidance techniques give the learner what might be called *knowledge of alternatives*, with the important proviso that the subject knows in advance which is the correct alternative. In two earlier experiments (Carr, 1921; von Wright, 1957) on visual guidance, described more fully in the next chapter, it emerged that showing the learner the full range of possibilities gave better results than merely showing him the correct path. These findings give us a clue towards assembling a great deal of what has gone before.

We began by considering how far reducing errors might contribute to learning. However, if this is done in such a way as to reduce the information available to the learner the learning will suffer. Knowledge of the correct response is incomplete if there is no opportunity to define it against the alternatives, just as we cannot be said to understand "red" if we have never identified other colours. On the other hand, Kaess and Zeaman's (1960) experiment, described earlier, suggests that it is inefficient to present the learner with a number of possibilities without indicating which of them is correct. Giving both correct and incorrect alternatives while ensuring correct responses seems to be the best solution.

In the two visual studies (Carr, 1921; von Wright, 1957), giving information about incorrect alternatives was an improvement. Similarly, Koch's animals learned well, having a view of the incorrect alley through a glass partition; her discrepant results with humans have already been considered. Naturally, knowledge of alternatives may be acquired before guidance is given, with some benefit. For this reason, Ludgate's (1924) results were better after some unguided trials had provided contrast. Again, purely kinaesthetic guidance (Melcher, 1934; Holding, 1959) was relatively poor if given at the outset, but not when interspersed with free activity (Lincoln, 1956).

Of course, mere knowledge of the alternatives to the correct response need not encourage errors, as might appear at first sight. Kaess and Zeaman (1960), for instance, whose work on punchboard learning has been described, showed that merely reading wrong answers did not fixate them as errors. On the other hand, if the wrong answers were actually punched then later unlearning was needed. It is easy to see, therefore, that the methods of visual guidance lend themselves readily to the presentation of incorrect alternatives; but we might imagine that the danger of error learning prohibits the giving of extra information by the physical methods of guidance. Forcing a subject to commit an "error" might be undesirable. However, a subject guided into an alternative response pattern has not made a mistake—he has merely practised a response slightly different from the one finally required. Thus, the apparent success of guiding a range of movements, including both correct and "incorrect" items (Waters, 1931; Macrae and Holding, in press), also falls into place.

It is clear, too, why training by knowledge of results is often preferred. At the expense of some errors, knowledge of alternatives is acquired automatically, becoming more precise as the correct response is neared, by successive discrimination. However, it is possible to build knowledge of alternatives into guidance procedures and, as we have seen, these techniques may often considerably shorten the course of learning.

SUMMARY

The fact that efficient performance depends upon knowledge of results does not imply that all learning must take place by trial-and-error. The methods of physical, visual and verbal guidance are all directed towards limiting the learning of errors which must later be eradicated. The present chapter reviews the evidence on the physical methods of restriction and forced-response.

Forced-response. In these methods the trainer takes complete charge of the response. Thus the exact form of the guided response is probably critical, although this has not received attention. In humans there is substantial learning of mazes and some benefit to discrete and continuous adjustive tasks. When the forced response is in conflict with the response finally required the restriction technique is more effective.

Restriction. Here the learner initiates and controls the speed and force of the response under spatial guidance. Restriction is effective in maze learning and in adjustive tasks. No direct comparisons with forced-response are available except in discrete adjustive skills, where restriction compares favourably with knowledge of results. Reversing the required movement favours forced-response.

Amount and position. Early conclusions recommending small amounts of guidance in the first stages of learning are not really borne out by the data, which show the issue to be rather complex. There is no doubt that for practical purposes guidance will often be used to teach the basic requirements, leaving final learning to the action of knowledge of results if only because the necessary refinements to guidance methods would be uneconomic. Some preliminary experience of unguided trials seems desirable.

Alternatives. Training by guidance methods may restrict the information offered to the learner by withholding knowledge of alternatives. When this difficulty is not overcome by preliminary experience or the design of the task explicit practice with alternatives may be given. A learner practising alternatives is not learning errors if he knows which is the correct response.

4. VISUAL METHODS

THERE are various ways of showing the learner what to do. Besides giving various kinds of visual guidance, we can modify the visual parts of a training task in several ways, or act out the necessary operations for imitation by the learner, or provide a multitude of visual aids.

It is not always easy to sort research into neat piles, and the visual methods do form an untidy assortment. However, it is possible to impose some order by noticing that these methods vary in the closeness with which they are tied to the task to be learned. The techniques of visual guidance, for instance, have a very direct effect upon performance, since the visual components of the task itself are modified. Demonstrating how to execute a dance step is intermediate; additional visual information is conveyed to which the learner does not respond directly, but by imitation. Films, too, may provide a basis for imitation. Laying out a periodic table of the elements is comparatively remote from the operations carried out by a physical chemist; tables, charts and similar visual aids present condensed, symbolic information and, of course, they are less often relevant to motor learning.

VISUAL GUIDANCE

Having earlier surveyed the evidence on the physical forms of guidance, we should next consider the visual guidance experiments. These raise similar problems of principle, although the kind of guidance which they offer is less definite. They provide *indication* rather than *constraint*. In fact, the kinds of visual indication which may be properly considered "guidance" are not easy to specify.

Experiments in this area have taken several forms, although a common theme is the provision of a spatial pathway to guide response.

An early example (Gates and Taylor, 1923) concerns the direct following of spatial paths, as against the following of separated paths; in other words, tracing and copying. Kindergarten children were taught to write letters of the alphabet by these two methods for several days, and then tested for free writing. Apparently, copying was far more effective than tracing; although it is difficult to assess these results, since the score included the quantity of letters produced as well as a measure of their quality. The tracing activity was slow, painstaking and wobbly; its practitioners are probably best regarded as receiving immediate, visual knowledge of results, as much as guidance, whenever the pencil deviated from the line. Therefore, despite better results during learning, its removal will bring a deterioration. In any case, the movements made during training are dissimilar from those required on test, which handicaps any training for graded skills.

The actual form of movement is of little account in maze-learning, where Carr (1921) investigated learning with and without vision. He constructed a grooved maze, in which blind alleys were marked by studs set low and out of sight. This allowed subjects to practise while seeing the pattern of the maze, but gave no visual indication of the true path. This is not therefore error-free guidance. After preliminary trials with vision, a screen was inserted, and they continued to learn in the normal way. The number of trials taken to learn the maze, including the visual ones, became fewer as the number of training trials increased; a result contradictory to Carr's (1930) conclusion. Two trials inserted as the fifth and sixth, when some learning had already occurred, were better than two initial trials. Inspecting the maze for one minute before beginning the learning trials, by the way, made the scores worse.

A second experiment raises the question of the amount of information presented by guidance. This time, subjects found their way through the maze with the aid of diagrams. There were three such diagrams. One depicted all the pathways, but omitted the stops from the blind alleys. Another diagram showed both pathways and stops, while a third showed only the true path. Essentially the same procedure was later used by von Wright (1957), who devised a kind of maze-tracking task. The maze paths travelled towards the subject on a strip of paper, and he attempted to follow the true path with a stylus. Only a part of the pattern was visible at any one time, through a small aperture. Again, as shown in Fig. 15, there were three conditions. Both paths, but not the stops, might be visible; or paths, and stops, might be visible; or only the true path was shown.

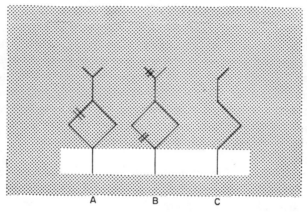

FIG. 15. Three kinds of visual guidance. After von Wright (1957).

In both experiments, the version which gave the most information brought about the most rapid learning. Showing both the true path and the incorrect alternatives reduced both trials and errors greatly. The true path alone was the next most effective for the trials measured by von Wright, but only in terms of the error score in Carr's study. As we concluded in the previous chapter, knowledge of alternatives is useful in supplementing the guidance of correct responses.

CHANGES IN DISPLAY

Most tasks comprise a display, presenting perceptual information, and some form of control which the learner operates. In the work on visual guidance the visual display may be separated out and manipulated as a means of training. As we have seen, varying the kind of information given by the display may result in quite different rates of learning. This probably happens too when the visual display is shifted spatially with respect to the tactual and control components of the task.

Shifting the visual display is more often a way of changing the task to make it more suitable than a method of training, but there is some scattered information which bears on learning. One clue comes from the maze experiment which was considered in the last section by Carr (1921). Persons using a diagram which was placed to the left of the maze needed about eleven trials to find their way through without errors. By contrast, learning to the same standard while seeing the maze pattern directly needed only three trials with vision. This effect must have been largely due to the spatial separation of the diagram from the maze.

Spatial separation may be varied very neatly in the lights-and-keys type of task, where Morin and Grant (1955) showed that the level of performance depends directly upon the degree of relationship between the elements of display and control. Performance is better if the lights are in the same order as the keys, and declines as they tend to be out of order or in the opposite order. Of course, if the correspondence is not spatial at all, but symbolic, the task may be made very difficult indeed. Kay (1954) showed this by requiring subjects to consult a coding card in order to discover which key operated which light.

The display may also differ from the control element in its angle of orientation. Miles (1927) constructed a double maze with two identical patterns mounted one above the other. Rotating the lower maze relative to the visual display contributed by the upper one made tracing the lower maze progressively more difficult. In a more modern setting there has been a great deal of work on the display–control relations of knobs, levers and dials; Loveless (1962) has recently reviewed the accumulated literature. However, like much other work on skills, this kind of information bears more directly upon the design of tasks than upon the conduct of training.

VISUAL MAGNIFICATION

Sometimes the design of the task can be usefully altered so that a modified version is available for training purposes. An excellent example is provided by Belbin, Belbin and Hill (1957), investigating special methods in industrial training. In this case the problem was the mending of complicated cloth weaves (Fig. 16). The task was considered difficult, even by younger workers, and good eyesight was considered essential. However, a careful analysis showed that the

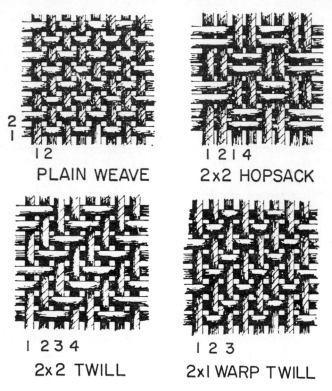

FIG. 16. Perceptual problems with several textile weaves. From Belbin, Belbin and Hill (1957).

problem of "seeing" was the problem of understanding what was needed, of seeing how the weaves were made up. This was a perceptual skill which presented inefficient visual cues to the learner. The experimenters therefore constructed large-scale weaves in which the interlacings, and the results of the trainees' own manoeuvres, were clearly visible. As skill was acquired the size of weave was gradually reduced to the normal proportions, aided at first by the use of industrial magnifiers.

The new training scheme was carefully evaluated against the two other methods in use in the textile mills. The traditional training was the familiar "sit by me" or exposure method, leaving the trainee to acquire the skill by observing an experienced operator. In addition, some supervisors were taught by T.W.I. (Training Within Industry) methods to carry out the training of operatives. These methods rely upon a moderately systematic breakdown of jobs into part tasks which are practised separately.

After twelve weeks' training it was possible to compare test mends made by trainees in the three groups. Differences in the quality of the mends were slight, although favouring the magnification trainees, who were able to complete some mends which were impossible for those in the other two groups. The average time needed to perform a mend was lower after the special training; this was true both for the weaves on which they had been trained and for new weaves. There was less variation in final ability within the group—the other two groups finishing with a mixture of good and bad menders. Later the method was used with older workers newly entering the textile industry (Belbin, 1958), with whom it proved highly effective. Inexperienced housewives learned in three to six hours to perform at speeds which girls under traditional methods took weeks to reach.

IMITATION

"Sit by me" training depends largely upon imitation, as do more formal kinds of demonstration. Since such methods have been widely used for a very long time it is perhaps surprising that so little research on imitation has been undertaken, and that so little is known about the factors which make for its success or failure.

Learning by imitation is clearly possible. If evidence were needed, Twitmyer's (1931) demonstration might suffice. This was derived from the familiar maze-learning setting and purported to show the effects of visual guidance, although in this kind of work both the visual and the motor sides of the task are replaced during training. Quite simply, one group of subjects stood and watched while the other group practised traversing a stylus maze. Although the passively learning group had not been warned that they would have to learn the maze themselves, they began at a level of performance three times as fast as the control group. Their subsequent learning was not as rapid, but after ten trials they equalled the performance that the control group showed when they had completed fifteen trials by the end of the session.

Merely observing others practise can have other interesting effects, which may be quite concrete. Hellebrandt and Waterland (1962) have reported a measurable influence on the relevant muscle groups of observers watching others exercise. Adams (1955) showed that watching other people work makes one demonstrably tired. The work in this case was following a dot on a gramophone turntable—the repetitive "pursuit rotor" task. What happened was that scores after a normal rest pause were higher than when the rest interval was spent in watching another person tracking. The fact that fatigue can occur is clearly linked to the fact that learning can occur.

Miller and Dollard (1941) suggest a distinction between "matched-dependent" behaviour and copying. In matched-dependent behaviour the imitator relies for perceptual cues upon the behaviour of a leader or demonstrator. Many children's activities, and the actions of crowds, are often performed in this way without insight into the cues determining the behaviour of the leaders. In "copying" the learner attempts to match the behaviour of a model, but by relating his actions to the appropriate environmental cues and clearly comparing his responses with those of the instructor. The difference is between doing what the leader does and learning how to do what the leader does. It seems consequently that learning *when* to carry out known sequences is characteristic of matched-dependency whereas copying, in this sense, occurs when new actions are to be learned. The copying process is therefore relevant to the problems of training.

In learning to copy the trainee begins by trying a response which appears similar to that of the instructor. More strictly the attempted response feels as if it will resemble the visual appearance of the instructor's response; or is selected because it promises to feel similar to what is assumed to be the feel of the instructor's response. In other words the production of an imitative response is a complex process, depending upon a learned correspondence between visual and kinaesthetic sensitivity. In all probability this learning is built up in the early years of one's life by the observation of one's own movements.

After his first attempts at copying a demonstrated movement the learner may perfect his response by trial-and-error. If the action has clearly identifiable consequences, as in laying a course of bricks, he can rely largely upon environmental knowledge of results in the form of extruding mortar and irregular placing of bricks, rather than upon gleaning further information from the instructor. In fact it is important that he should rely upon permanently available cues for his later performance. As we saw when considering knowledge of results, it is unwise to rely heavily upon temporary, supplementary cues.

A simple experiment by Miller and Dollard (1941) makes this plain. Some children were trained to imitate, and others not to imitate, an experimental leader. It was arranged, for some, that the leader opened a box containing a bright light to obtain sweets. For others he opened an alternative, dark box. Next the sweets were placed in whichever box had previously been empty and the children were required to find the sweets. The percentage figures for those who did are shown in Table 2. When imitating had the effect of exposing children to the critical cue—the light in the box—the imitators did better than the others. When imitating led them to the dark box the non-imitators profited from finding that the illuminated box was empty. Whether or not imitation was successful depended upon the opportunity to perceive the relevant environmental cue.

TABLE 2. Percentage of children making the correct choice. (After Miller and Dollard, 1941)

	Sweet in light box	Sweet in dark box
Imitators	90*	30
Non-imitators	40	100*

* Exposed to the critical cue

Not all behaviour has obvious results. If the action is an end in itself, as in ballet, the learner is forced to rely upon his perception of sameness and differences in his own and the instructor's performance. Very often the instructor will supply verbal knowledge of results, but gradually the learner must refine his own standards of judgment. In any case the learning will continue along the familiar lines of trial-and-error; the special contribution of imitation lies in enormously reducing the field of possible responses when learning begins.

For this very reason the value of imitation may often be under-estimated. In a comparison of imitative, or exposure, methods with other forms of training much of the work of imitation may have been already accomplished before training proper is under way. It is seldom that a trainee begins an operation without first seeing it performed. This means that the range of appropriate actions is narrowed down, and that attention is already drawn to the timing of responses and to critical perceptual cues. The consequent reduction of sources of error will benefit any ensuing form of training.

STATIC VISUAL AIDS

The next point to consider is how far training should be supplemented by additional visual materials. There is no magic about visual aids. They are effective where they are appropriate. It would be idle to deny that well-designed visual data properly integrated into a training scheme may assist learning, but any advantages they have derive from the same principles of learning already described. Unfortunately, visual gadgets, like illuminated charts and brightly coloured models, possess what psychologists call "face validity"; that is to say they have an immediate, superficial appeal which is not necessarily justified, but which tends to generate enthusiasm among their sponsors.

There is no doubt that it may sometimes be essential to present information pictorially. The teaching of aircraft recognition, for instance, is almost impossible without visual material. However, the value of pictures which supplement a verbal text is open to doubt. Vernon (1953) tested the remembering by older school children of articles on various diseases, presented with and without pictures or graphs. Neither kind of visual material significantly affected the total amount of coherence of what was remembered. Even with younger children, to whom pictures might be expected to appeal, illustrations gave no assistance (Vernon, 1954). Certain factual points were better remembered from pictures, having received special emphasis, but at the expense of other material. There was in any case a general tendency to distort the material and to omit the explanatory statements.

TABLE 3. Percentage of features remembered with
and without graphs. (After Vernon, 1951)

	Important facts	Explanations
Graphs	37	49
No Graphs	54	62

Similar tendencies were clearly marked in another experiment on graphs (Vernon, 1951). This time passages were used dealing with birth and death rates, and with the relation of disease to living conditions. In general the recall of material from the written text alone was smoother and more coherent than when graphs were used. Table 2 shows that the graphs interfered with the remembering of important items of information and, what is more, reduced the number of essential steps in the argument which were grasped. Doubtless if graphs are to be of use the readers must be of appropriate age and intelligence, and must make a real attempt to incorporate the graphical material into the logical structure of the text.

Graphs do have the advantage of displaying trends—a rise or a fall or a more complicated relationship are easily shown—and they make it easy to find readings interpolated between the values which are marked. Yet if exact readings are needed, with no interpolations, tables are more efficient than graphs (Chapanis, Garner and Morgan, 1949).

It should be borne in mind that the memorizing experiments may not give us the whole story. The use which people make of pictorial information, and their ability to remember what they have seen, may be separate functions. Experiments which are described in the next chapter suggest that, at least with some people, knowledge may be directly incorporated into behaviour rather than shown as verbal remembering. However, the state of the current evidence on visual aids enjoins some caution in their use.

MOVING FILMS

Obviously the value of a film depends upon its content. A film or a television programme used as a recorded lecture is no more effective than the lecture itself, unless advantage is taken of special techniques like slow motion sequences and animated diagrams. After a three-year interval lecture material is remembered equally well whether presented live or by television (Benschoter and Charles, 1957).

Used to teach manipulative skills the film may provide a basis for imitative learning, and may be used to set a standard towards which knowledge of results may be directed in practice. Here it is possible to arrange that the trainee will see the operation as he would perform it himself, using the "camera behind operator" technique, whereas in a live demonstration it often happens that the learner sees the operation in reverse. Roshal compared the effects of the two directions of camera angle, giving "right way round" or "back to front" views, in films teaching trainees to tie sheet bends and bowline knots (Gagné and Fleishman, 1959). His findings confirm the superiority of aligning the camera with the operator's line of sight. Also it appeared that the factor of movement was important, the results with motion shots being more successful than training by static film strips.

Movement of the film may be less important in procedural skills, where operations fall naturally into separate units. At all events no real differences emerged in Laner's (1954) study of film and filmstrip training. The task here was the dismantling, repair and reassembly of a sash-cord window. Both the film, and its static version, used the same spoken commentary. The greatest difficulty and the most errors seemed to occur during the repair stage and it was here, if anywhere, that the continuity afforded by the moving film tended to prove an advantage. As often happens when long procedural sequences are presented only once, operations were frequently carried out in the wrong order. Serial learning requires repeated practice, so that the single showing usually given to films must be held a disadvantage.

As a further assessment of the moving film in technical instruction Laner (1955) compared an explanatory text with a film showing the operation of a Bren gun trigger mechanism. This was a severe test, since the mechanism was complicated and unfamiliar, and could only be understood if the interaction of its moving parts were appreciated. The text, based again upon the sound track, contained only two diagrams. After training subjects were asked to sketch the parts, to answer questions designed to reveal their understanding of the mechanism, and finally to assemble a dismantled trigger.

Again the performance scores of the two groups were equivalent. Seeing the film seemed to confer no special knowledge or facility upon the viewers. All the subjects managed to assemble the mechanism, although the time they needed for this depended less upon the kind of training they received than upon the understanding shown by their answers to the questions (Fig. 17). Most subjects approved of the film, but any advantage it may have conferred was

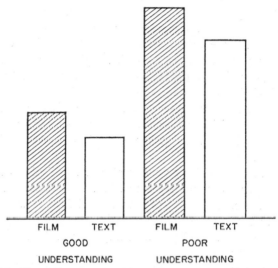

Fig. 17. Time taken to assemble a trigger mechanism after instruction by film or text. After Laner (1955).

nullified by its inflexibility. The presentation was paced, so that viewers had no control over the speed at which information was to be absorbed, and the film was irreversible. Subjects having the text were able to proceed at their own speed and to check back where necessary. While these facilities are denied to film users we may expect the advantage gained by continuity to be marginal.

On the other hand a factor which can make a larger practical difference to film learning is audience participation. Having the audience actively review the contents of a film section by section, so that the film is effectively incorporated in a systematic training scheme, is a clear advantage over passive viewing (Michael and Maccoby, 1953). As we might expect, giving knowledge of results is particularly effective. When the audience replies to questions covering successive parts of the film, the same study shows that learning is enhanced by giving the correct answers.

SUMMARY

There are three main kinds of visual change or addition which the trainer can use. (1) He can change the display part of the task so that more efficient motor actions ensue (visual guidance, changes in position or orientation, magnification). (2) He can instead provide a complete visual display which depicts the necessary actions (demonstrations, films). (3) He can provide extra visual material of a symbolic kind (charts, diagrams, films).

Display changes. We have seen that *visual guidance* is a useful and flexible method of indicating the correct response and that it is possible and desirable to adapt the method to displaying alternatives at the same time.

Changes in the *position* or *orientation* of the display with respect to the control movements seem to affect the efficiency of learning and performance. However, the most usual form of task has direct spatial correspondence, which is the best arrangement, so that these changes will seldom be of practical importance. If the task is "out of alignment" the best remedy is to change the task.

Where a task presents perceptual difficulties *magnifying* the whole task allows the learner to see clearly what is to be done, and to get clear knowledge of results magnified to the same degree. Presumably the opposite process of "minifying" a task is appropriate if the perceptual demands are too wide—this may be one advantage of models like the globe or the planetarium—although there is no directly relevant evidence.

Demonstration. Apart from drawing attention to important perceptual cues, demonstrations and films show the learner what he is required to do, thus setting a standard against which he can compare his own efforts. They also provide a basis for *imitation*. Little research has been devoted to imitation, but it is clear that some imitative learning is possible. Imitation is probably best used to narrow down the field for later trial-and-error learning and should be supplemented by more efficient techniques.

Visual aids. Pictures, graphs and charts may break a text into more assimilable portions or add some variety to a lecture course, and with some readers may be the only way of ensuring that the text is read at all. However what evidence there is gives little support for the widespread use of visual aids. The existing research may not be adequate, but it is evident that claims for the importance of visual aids need more rigorous experimental support.

The use of *films* is a potential way of obtaining a condensed record of the best available visual and verbal training items, but again falls short of its promise in the light of present evidence. The impression of movement conveyed by a film may or may not be important. Any advantage due to continuity is offset by the film's irreversibility and its presentation of information at a fixed rate. Supplementing a film by question and answer procedures is better than allowing passive viewing.

5. WORDS AND ACTIONS

WORDS and symbols enter into every phase of human training. Before practice begins the trainer may give verbal instructions, or he may require the learner to undertake preliminary practice with words, as "verbal pre-training". During practice he may assist with verbal guidance or hints. Following practice he may, as we have already seen, correct the learner's performance by verbal knowledge of results. If the trainer does not introduce words and symbols before, during or after practice the learner will. Muttering to oneself, silently or aloud, helps in grouping broad classes of stimuli or in fixing subtle distinctions; self-praise or blame strengthens or selects among responses; plans of action may be outlined and evaluated internally; tendencies to respond in one way may be replaced through verbal linkage by tendencies to respond in another, physically unrelated way.

VERBAL AND MOTOR LEARNING

In previous chapters free use has been made of rather abstract terms like "response", or "performance", expressly because these terms do not distinguish between words and bodily actions. Despite the fact that the fields of verbal and motor learning are often treated for convenience as separate areas of investigation, the same principles of learning apply to both kinds of behaviour. After all, producing words is a form of muscular response, albeit of an extremely specialized and complex kind.

Just as we can strengthen, say, whisker-licking behaviour in the white rat, by selectively rewarding the response that we want to encourage, we can reinforce the parts of speech that we want a human subject to use. Greenspoon (1955) discovered that saying "mmm-hmm" after any plural noun, like "cigars" or "smiles" or "superstitions", made people produce many more such plurals without being given any explicit instructions. Verplanck (1955) obtained similar effects, even over the telephone, in encouraging people to vouchsafe statements of opinion. In the early work it appeared unimportant whether or not subjects were aware of the reinforcement, although it is now clear (De Nike and Spielberger, 1963) that such awareness may bring complications.

There are many other parallels between motor and symbolic learning. The general similarities need not be laboured, but it is of interest to examine some points of detailed resemblance. Like long verbal sequences, long sequences of motor responses are easiest at the beginning and end (Neumann and Ammons, 1957); as we saw in the last chapter muddles may occur over the middle items, and these are only overcome by repetitive practice. Again, getting off to a bad start seems to affect both in the same way. Welford, Brown and Gabb (1950) tested the crews of civil aircraft, tired after protracted flying, and showed that the impairment in their motor performance persisted when they were tested again after complete rest. Broadbent's (1958b) findings in a symbolic task are similar. Practising a mental arithmetic task for the first time in noise left after-effects which persisted in later quiet conditions.

Forgetting, too, probably affects both classes of response in the same way, although the evidence here is more complicated. There are plenty of examples of long-term retention in motor skills. That we can remember how to skate, or to ride a bicycle, for months and years is traditional knowledge; while an instance of documentary evidence is provided by Johnson (1927), who recorded successful tightrope walking after a break of two years. Since there are plenty of instances of verbal *forgetting* it is often assumed that motor learning is somehow more permanent by its very nature. This is not true, but there are several reasons why verbal forgetting occurs more often.

In the first place, how well something is remembered depends upon how well it is learned. Most motor sequences are highly overlearned, practised well beyond the point of mastery. Verbal sequences are usually not, although we can probably all remember well-rehearsed instructions or snatches of poetry, which come back to us just as readily as disused skills like hopscotch or marbles. Thus only an experiment in which the amount of original learning is controlled can give a clear idea as to whether there are any real differences between retaining words and movements.

A further consideration is that verbal sequences often carry more information and thus present the brain with a greater storage load. This occurs partly because of the wide range of meanings available, partly because verbal sequences typically come in longer stretches between external cues—in sentences rather than in discrete responses—and partly because in motor sequences one response often provides a relatively unambiguous cue to the next. If both the prior learning and the difficulty of the motor and verbal tasks are balanced by careful experimental design, then differences in their retention disappear (Van Dusen and Schlosberg, 1948).

VERBAL AND MOTOR BEHAVIOUR

It appears that verbal learning and motor learning have many features in common despite their superficial differences. Of course there are often extra complexities in verbal learning, since the inter-relationships between words are many and various. Further, in verbal learning one is most often concerned with the rearrangement of existing verbal responses, whereas motor learning commonly requires the acquisition or adaptation of new responses. This is the distinction between serial, or procedural, learning and skill learning. In fact, serial learning may occur in verbal or in motor tasks, while most skill learning is in non-verbal activities. An obvious exception to this generalization is in learning a new language, where phonetic difficulties may necessitate prolonged learning of a single new word. The fact that words can "mean" motor responses, and that motor responses can evoke words, further complicates a description of the two types of behaviour.

It is important to bear in mind that these are two types of behaviour which, though related, are separate. We cannot adequately describe all that we do, and we cannot do all that we can describe. As Broadbent (1958a) points out, we can usually show that we have absorbed a given amount of information by making a verbal response, or else by making a bodily response, but not necessarily both. We can for instance direct people to a strange address by giving a list of directions and street names or by taking them there, although the fact that one method is possible does not automatically guarantee that we can carry out the other.

Reporting verbally on what we can do bodily is an extra activity superimposed on the motor responses; it is quite unreasonable to suppose that this extra activity is always appropriate, or that the required extra capacity is always there. It is in this sense that many of our activities are unconscious, which merely means that we cannot report on them very well. Of course, some further difficulties in the idea of "the unconscious" are due instead to the hazy status of motives. Motives are not the kind of things which can be inspected and judged—they are inferred, even by their owners. Hence it is not surprising that the inferences about human motives made by an impartial observer are sometimes nearer the mark than the guesses one makes oneself.

Although verbal learning and motor learning are affected similarly by the factors which determine serial or skilled performance, we cannot jump to the conclusion that verbal and motor responses are always equivalent. No one doubts that people can often learn a list of simple instructions and then translate them into action. In fact this is a very common and effective way of learning many procedural skills. On the other hand, if we measure what people have learned in two different ways the levels of verbal and motor ability which they display may be different. Belbin (1956) allowed people of various ages to see safety posters and then tested their knowledge in two ways. One consisted of getting verbal descriptions of the posters, the other of examining the use made of the safety information in analysing faults in problem photographs. The photographs showed a range of local traffic scenes, involving pedestrians, cyclists, cars and policemen.

Among the many results of this experiment it appeared that although younger subjects did better at verbal *recall* of the information, the *use* scores of the older subjects were, if anything, higher. The safety advice was more directly incorporated into the behaviour of the over-sixties, although they would have shown a decline in a written examination.

Such a finding suggests that different training procedures with less stress upon symbolic learning might be more appropriate for older workers. This idea was tested by Belbin (1958) in a comparison

of memorization with "activity training". The first experiment was
in the form of a sorting task. Fifty numbered cards had to be
"posted" into coloured slots, and the relation between number and
colour had to be learned so that cards could be posted quickly and
accurately.

In the memorization method the subject was left to learn the
relations between numbers and colours from a tabulated chart. All

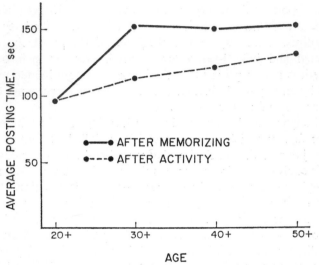

FIG. 18.   Greater efficiency of "activity" learning for a sorting task.
After Belbin (1958).

numbers in the twenties, for instance, were allocated to pink slots,
the thirties being assigned to black. When the subject was satisfied
that he had learned the relationships a verbal test of his knowledge
was administered. The activity method consisted of practice in
sorting, a kind of visual guidance being provided by making the
practice cards of the appropriate colours.

The sorting job was carried out more quickly after activity
training (Fig. 18), and also with greater accuracy. However, the
time taken to learn by memorizing was considerably shorter, so a
second experiment was designed to eliminate the effects of this and
several other factors. In this version numbers were correlated with
slot positions rather than with colours; the score recorded was the

time taken to reach a given sorting speed, including both preliminary learning time and the time spent in practising the task. As Fig. 19 shows, learning by bodily activity was more efficient with the older subjects, despite the slight advantage of the memorization method for the young.

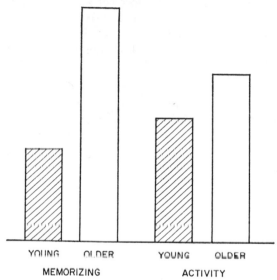

FIG. 19. Times taken to learn a sorting task. Although younger subjects tend to find memorizing quicker, older subjects do better with "activity" training. After Belbin (1958).

In all probability this contrast in efficiency between training methods applies to groups of differing ability and education, as well as to different age groups. University students, a highly verbal group, seem to prefer the memorization method; persons holding academic posts were found to impose the technique of memorization upon the activity training, thus spoiling its effect.

INSTRUCTIONS

It appears therefore that the giving of detailed verbal instructions may sometimes be less advisable than is implied by their widespread use in training, since not all learners are equally ready to learn a task by verbal methods. Instructions form a verbal load which must be carried throughout an activity, in addition to the changing demands of the task itself. Translating words into actions is a further process, itself requiring attention, so that the capacity of an operator may easily be exceeded. The serial learning of procedures may be more suited to verbal methods than a complicated adjustive skill.

It is possible to disrupt the operator's performance in quite a lasting way by the over-elaboration of instructions. An early experiment on pursuit tracking (Renshaw and Postle, 1928) makes this clear. Merely telling subjects to keep the apparatus running pro-

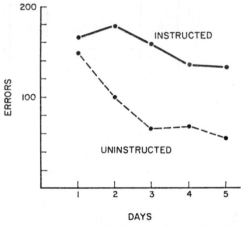

FIG. 20. Adverse effect of detailed instructions. After Renshaw and Postle (1938).

duced results as good as did encouraging them to record and analyse their performance, and far better than a detailed set of instruction. These last were preceded by a demonstration, and explained the best ways of operating the mechanism and of overcoming known difficulties. The unfortunate consequences of this procedure are emphasized by the fact that the early differences in learning tended to become wider as training progressed. During the first day's tracking the uninstructed group were slightly better, but by the fifth day their scores were about three times as good as those of the subjects carrying a heavy burden of instructions (Fig. 20).

Clearly the effect of instructions must depend both upon the form taken by the instructions and upon the nature of the task. Detailed handling instructions may be confusing in a motor task, where the enunciation of a simple principle might have greater effect. However, even the effect of a simple statement of principle may be found equivocal. In Judd's (1908) famous experiment, where one of two groups throwing darts at a submerged target was given preliminary instruction in the principles of light refraction, initial performance was unaffected.

It was only when the target was shifted to a different depth that the instructed group appeared to benefit; while even this conclusion has been challenged by Colville (1957), who showed that an equivalent amount of time spent in practising games skills produced the same effects as explaining the relevant simple mechanics. Kresse, Peterson and Grant (1954) found little difference between conceptual instructions, which explained a radar display in terms of the movements of the radar aerial and of the aircraft appearing on the screen, and practical instructions which merely dealt with the use of the controls.

In a problem-solving situation, where a single principle is a complete key to the solution, it would be easy to suppose that instructions could completely replace practice. However, Waters (1928) experimented with a form of the game "nim", in which the object was to draw one or two beads from a pile in such a way as to win the last bead from an opponent, comparing several kinds of preliminary instruction with different techniques of learning by practice. The best method was to make the subject call out after each draw how many beads were left, thus drawing his attention to the most relevant cue to success. Next in effectiveness came the most concrete form of instructions, "always draw so as to leave a multiple of three", although this rule did not apply to later problems. More abstract formulations like "always draw so as to leave a multiple of the sum of the highest and lowest possible draws" did not succeed despite the fact that they applied to all the problems which were set. Evidently, any instructions must be simple and direct.

This point is underlined by Conrad (1962), who carried out a test of the printed instruction card which is supplied for use with an internal telephone network. Faced with the job of transferring an outside call from one extension to another, without going through the central office, only four of a group of twenty subjects succeeded in using the standard instruction card. The card presents a large mass of printed instructions, among which are imbedded three sentences critical to the transfer of call manoeuvre. The first two are separated from the third by nine lines of print referring to other operations. Two improved versions of the instruction card were produced, a shortened form containing only the relevant sentences and a re-worded version in which the three parts of the instruction were clearly located together. Both of these cards brought about an improvement, fourteen or fifteen subjects out of twenty now being able to carry out the operation.

PRE-DIFFERENTIATION

Actually practising words, instead of receiving verbal instructions from the trainer, may have effects which persist in the learning of a motor skill. Verbal pre-training techniques, as these methods of preliminary word practice are called, are in quite common use. Children are taught to rehearse "stop, look and listen, before you cross the street" on the assumption that this verbal performance will transfer its effects to an equivalent motor performance at the kerbside. Recruits are taught to name the parts of a machine-gun down to the last split-pin on the assumption that the acquired discrimination will be of use in handling the weapon.

One factor which appears to be important in training of this kind is the effect of learning words upon the subject's ability to handle the task stimuli. Perceptual cues which are difficult to discriminate, like fingerprints or lights of varying brightness, often seem to acquire distinctiveness when they are given verbal labels (Arnoult, 1957). Classifying nonsense shapes, for instance, is better accomplished when subjects learn appropriate labels for the shapes (Pfafflin, 1960), although the labels are a disadvantage with clearly identifiable silhouettes. It is probably important that the verbal labels are strongly linked to the stimuli, either by virtue of their meaning or, if they are nonsense syllables or letters, by a high degree of learning (Goss, 1953; De Rivera, 1959).

It may not be immediately clear that giving names to things helps us to tell them apart or, as it is said, that "stimulus predifferentiation" takes place. Perhaps the simplest way to think about the pre-differentiation process is as if one were daubing a set of similar objects with a variety of imaginary colours in order to set them apart more clearly. When objects really do differ physically in more than one way they are certainly easier to separate; and provided that the added physical dimension is psychologically linked to the first, as are for instance one's judgments of taste and smell, they are more easily arranged in a series.

Anthony and others (1962) showed that it is possible literally to extend or contract a subject's scale of judgments by varying the sizes of a set of weights, although only weight was to be judged. Similar effects occur when the extra dimension is one of value, rather than a physical characteristic, as Tajfel (1957) has explained. Objects which are valuable tend to seem more different one from another than do neutral objects. Thus, poor children tend to overestimate the sizes of valuable coins (Carter and Schooler, 1949) and jars of sweets seem heavier than jars of sand (Dukes and Bevan, 1952). Value is quite as abstract as a verbal label, so that it is not unreasonable to expect associated words to increase discrimination, although an explanation along these lines is undoubtedly an over-simplification.

VERBAL PRE-TRAINING

When verbal pre-training techniques are used to prepare a subject for a manipulative task, the method is usually to present letters or words alongside the stimuli to be used in the later task. In the case of Gagné and Baker (1950) the stimuli were coloured lights in various positions, and subjects learned to associate these with arbitrary letters before going on to practise the main task; this consisted merely of pressing the appropriate switch when each of the stimulus lights was shown. As depicted in Fig. 21, the verbal procedure did facilitate performance on the main task, the greatest benefit deriving from the longest pre-training. Given sufficient training, once can also learn effectively with words substituted for the stimuli of the main task (Baker and Wylie, 1950).

Teaching verbal responses to the task stimuli, while often beneficial, may bring complications. The trouble is that the verbally trained subject, faced with those same stimuli in the main task, has two potential responses—one verbal and one motor. He may have been taught to say "zop" when a red light shines, but is now required to wind a handle instead. In some instances the verbal response will help the motor response, but the two responses may and sometimes do compete. The resulting interference may produce errors or increase the time taken to make a response. Of course this is most likely to happen if the response word does not mean the motor response, so that the subject is trying to think "petroleum jelly" and do "three inches to the right and one forward". Thinking "press" and doing "press" is far less troublesome.

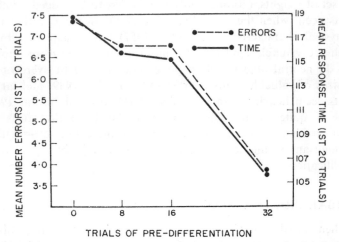

FIG. 21. Improvement in time and error scores as a result of verbal pre-training. From Gagné and Baker (1950).

Something of this kind occurred in an experiment by McAllister (1953). Subjects were to move a joystick into one of the six arms of a star pattern in accordance with stimuli of different colours. For one kind of pre-training the colours were linked with irrelevant words, so that orange went with "haggard", purple with "uncouth" and white with "sullen"; for another group of subjects the colours were linked with relevant words which indicated the required responses. Compared with a control group the relevant group began the motor task with better scores whereas, as we have foreseen, the group who learned irrelevant words were worse off. A further finding in the same experiment concerned the form taken by the relevant words, some of which were far more effective than others. Movements of the joystick could easily be represented by the analogy of a clock, as "twelve o'clock, eight o'clock" and so on, or else by directions like "forward" or "left-backward". Both these kinds of response word were superior to a geometric description like "0 degrees" or "240 degrees".

In a similar study McCormack (1958) found that the learning of meaningful adjectives could be a hindrance to persons beginning the manipulative task, when the previous verbal learning was stopped at a critical stage. Battig (1954) investigated a more complicated, two-dimensional task, in which joystick movements were directed by rows and columns of thirteen lights. If verbal directions were substituted for the *stimulus* lights during pre-training the subjects improved. Again, however, practising a verbal *response* was disadvantageous, even though this took the form of allowing the subject to describe how he would have moved the joystick had he been using it.

The existing evidence is incomplete and is mainly restricted to simple manipulative tasks, but it seems possible to summarize the above and other findings in the following way. Pre-training with verbal responses is useful if the verbal material takes the form of relatively neutral letters or nonsense syllables, or if the words used mean the responses in a simple, direct fashion. It is at least consistent with this conclusion that Goss and Greenfield (1958) found equal facilitation by nonsense syllables as by simple words coined by the experimenter or his subject to describe varying intensities of light. If, on the other hand, the words are elaborate, or if they have a meaning which is unrelated to the motor response or, worse still, antagonistic to the motor response, it is probable that learning will suffer.

VERBAL GUIDANCE AND HINTS

Whether or not they are taught verbal responses, people tend in any case to mutter to themselves, particularly through the early stages of practice. The muttering appears to guide their responses and it is natural to try to capitalize on this by having them call out their instructions stage by stage. This appears more direct than prior verbal learning, but has not been shown to help. Lawshe and Cary (1952) had learners talking back instructions as they assembled gears, levers and shafts during a practice trial, but this did not bring any improvement, though it is possible that a single trial was insufficient.

If the experimenter breaks up the instructions and spaces them out through the task we have what amounts to verbal guidance, which appears extremely efficient. Wang (1925) examined the traditional maze-learning task, calling directions like a lorry-driver's mate backing his driver into a confined space, and found a great deal of improvement. After verbal guidance of different amounts the number of trials needed to learn the maze was compared with the number required by an untrained control group. As Fig. 22 shows, at least ten unguided trials were saved by each of the varying amounts of guidance.

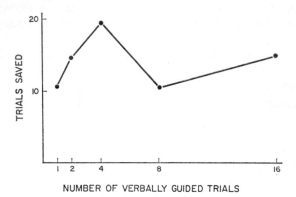

FIG. 22. The number of learning trials saved by verbal guidance. After Wang (1925).

In this experiment the words were again simple and directly relevant to the movements required: "turn to the left, keep going straight ahead, now turn right" and so on. It frequently happens with more elusive tasks that no words are available which would directly produce the necessary movements, which poses a practical training problem. There are many spatial arrangements which are awkward to verbalize coherently, so that it is notoriously difficult to describe a spiral staircase; similarly, verbal directions on speed of movement or the exertion of force are not easy to follow.

Not infrequently it is found that it pays to give figurative or emotive hints, rather than guidance which is to be interpreted literally. In falling short of the apparent aim of the trainer, or physically misconstruing his directions, the learner is led to perform in an adequate way. What matters of course is not the form of words, but the effect they produce. Cursing your drill squad causes resentment and, with luck, the resulting tendencies to expressive movement may be canalized into the energetic precision which distinguishes this form of group activity. The short-falling type of hint is best illustrated by the advice to young boxers: "aim your punch through your opponent's backbone". If, instead, the learner takes aim at the front of the ribs the normal deceleration of a controlled movement will result in a pulled punch.

In playing a piano the keys may be depressed with different degrees of force, and the time relations between notes and spaces may be varied. These are the only manual methods of achieving the entire range of possible styles and moods of play. Here, again, indirect verbal instructions are often appropriate. As Harrison (1958) explains, beauty of tone may often be achieved by oblique hints. Telling a child to "love the C-sharp" is effective, since it achieves the necessary delay in approaching and relinquishing the key. Many other effects, like "*legato*" or "*cantabile*", could be obtained by oblique verbal control of the appropriate movement sequences.

Discovering such verbal formulae is something of an art although, like all human behaviour, it is potentially susceptible to experimental analysis. One kind of relevant finding is illustrated by Münsterberg's (1892) early measurements of arm movements. Excitement tended to produce overshooting of a target length; depression brought about undershooting; while pleasure seemed to lengthen movements away from the body and to shorten movements towards the body. However, the existing science of hints and incitements is clearly rudimentary.

SUMMARY

Allowing for the usual differences between serial and skill learning, the same rules govern the learning of words and actions. However, verbal and motor activities are separate; what is learned verbally cannot always be translated into action, nor can learned actions always be put into words. In fact, people may remember information verbally or bodily, giving different scores for "recall" and "use".

Activity. Differences among people in verbal facility mean that "learning by doing" is often better than "learning by saying". While these differences have been demonstrated between older and

D

younger subjects, it is probable that they also arise between groups of different ability and background.

Instructions. If instructions are to be effective they should be neither too elaborate nor too abstract. Simple, practical directions give the best results.

Pre-training. In verbal pre-training we use "learning by saying" as a preparation for "learning by doing". Having the subject learn words instead of addressing him with them may be useful (1) if the words help him to make perceptual distinctions, and (2) if his verbal response does not interfere with his action. These conditions seem to obtain when the task involves several similar stimuli, and when the verbal response means the motor action or else is simple and neutral.

Verbal guidance. Instead of making a verbal response to the ordinary task stimuli, as in pre-training, the subject may practise the ordinary motor response to verbal stimuli from the trainer. This kind of verbal guidance is effective, at least for serial learning. It is also a way of sharing through the task what would otherwise constitute over-elaborate instructions if given at the beginning.

The best form of words to use is not necessarily the most accurate, but the one which results in the required response being made. Such hints may sometimes rely upon the emotive connotations of the words used.

6. PRACTICE

THE skilled man works smoothly, has plenty of time and is in complete control of his movements; the beginner, on the other hand, is harassed and jerky. The skilled performer at any task is able to anticipate the course of events. As a result of practice he knows what is coming because it has come many times before, not always in the same form, but as a variety of essentially similar events. Consequently his performance is unhurried and, within the limits of his training, flexible. He can change his responses because he knows what is likely to happen. Events are less surprising to him, as a result of practice; and during practice he has been able to discard inefficient responses.

LEARNING CURVES

In any practical training situation it is impossible to learn without practice. Not mere practice, of course; practice alone is insufficient, as preceding discussions of verbal and visual methods, knowledge of results and guidance have made plain. Occasionally, if the task is extremely simple and it is not required to distinguish between responses of different degrees of accuracy, such practice may be very short.

Simple associations may be learned in only one trial. After one telling a person may be able to repeat "bats are chiroptera" or to answer "krg" to the stimulus "pnz". Research into one-trial learning, begun by Rock (1957), is of theoretical importance because of the possibility that what appears to be gradual learning is in fact made up of many little bits of one-trial learning. However, overall progress in learning a complete list of associations or a motor skill is gradual, whatever the underlying mechanism.

Plotting the scores made by learners as practice continues in the form of a continuous graph gives what is known as a learning curve. In the typical learning curve one expects a trial-by-trial improvement, which tapers off as the limit of learning is reached, in the way already shown in Figs. 1, 3, 9 and 20. It may sometimes take a very long time before progress tapers off, although figures on really prolonged learning are seldom available from laboratory studies. In the industrial example shown as Fig. 23 improvement continues for three million trials spread over two years of practice.

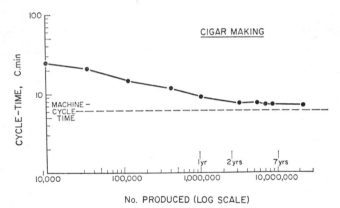

FIG. 23. Prolonged practice at cigar-making. From Crossman (1959).

Continued improvement with extended practice is by no means rare, and persistent training can sometimes bring unexpectedly high returns, as in teaching reading to the mentally backward (Gunzburg, 1948). Clarke and Hermelin (1955) undertook the training of imbeciles for industrial work like the soldering of television components, wire trimming to exact lengths and bicycle pump assembly. They propose that the main distinction between the performance of imbeciles and people of much higher intelligence depends less upon the final level of achievement in simple tasks than upon the amount of practice needed to achieve this level. With normal subjects extended practice tends to bring benefits in increased consistency of performance, exemplified in the steady cornering of skilled police drivers (Lewis, 1954), and increased resistance to interference from other learned material (McGeoch, 1929).

The slackening in apparent improvement which typifies the later stages of learning is sometimes mirrored by an early period in which little progress is made. With difficult tasks it is possible to obtain learning curves which gradually accelerate from a slow start (Krueger, 1947), instead of showing the deceleration which occurs with easier tasks. It seems probable that many learning curves would show both kinds of effect, with gains first increasing and later decreasing, if one began with completely unskilled subjects. Usually there is some prior skill and knowledge which the subject can bring to bear on the new task, thus curtailing the early stages of learning so that the initial increase in gains is not often seen.

Another kind of change in the course of learning is the "plateau" or temporary cessation in progress. The plateau was discovered by Bryan and Harter (1897) in learning to receive Morse code, and has since been more often discussed than observed. In the learning of code it appeared that there was a consolidating pause in receiving individual letters, which preceded the later stage of receiving whole words. Taylor (1943) showed that this behaviour was not the general rule; and in many laboratory learning curves, progress seems merely erratic rather than beset by plateaux. The performance of an individual subject tends to fluctuate for a number of reasons, and this is particularly marked when a complex skill is measured in an indirect way by a single score. No doubt it is often a matter of pure chance that several successive scores show no improvement and thus appear as a plateau.

SPEED AND ACCURACY

It is sometimes wondered whether practice is best carried out at speed with little initial stress upon accuracy, or whether more efficient learning results from gradually increasing the speed of initially accurate performance. There is little evidence of any lasting difference between these two procedures where they are applicable, while in a number of training situations it is doubtful whether the question has any real meaning. In the game of bowls, for instance, speed and accuracy are correlated; if the bowling movement is too fast or too slow, the missile will simply fail to come to rest in the appropriate place. Often at least a minimum speed is needed for any performance to take place and a higher speed makes accuracy easier, as in riding a bicycle.

In cases where accuracy may be sacrificed for speed of response, it has been suggested (Hovland, 1951) that two different situations may arise. In one case the form of the movement may remain unchanged at different speeds, as in typing. Otherwise, the operation may be substantially different when performed at high speed; bricklaying is a possible example. If this second situation does exist then clearly training at a low speed would be inefficient, since the learner would be practising an inappropriate task. However, even when high and low speed movements appear to differ in the

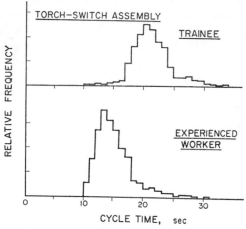

FIG. 24. The distribution of assembly times for a learner and an experienced worker. Based on data by N. A. Dudley; from Crossman (1959).

form they take they are probably both well inside the range of variation available to the learner.

Fulton (1945) failed to find any real advantage in speed training for a striking movement, where a difference might be expected. In a tracing task where movements are similar at varying speeds, it was possible to bias the performance of learners in favour of either speed or accuracy by the appropriate training. Other factors also influence the learner's preference for one or other aspect of performance; Welford (1958) describes tasks in which older persons typically stress accuracy at the expense of speed.

There is little doubt that speed can be built up gradually from a tolerably accurate response. What happens in a repetitive industrial task where only a "pass-or-fail" measure of accuracy is required is analysed by Crossman (1959). The performance of a trainee and an experienced worker are compared in Fig. 24, where the times taken for repeated assembling of torch switches are plotted. It is evident that the difference between the two operators lies in the distribution of times; that is to say, both men have a similar range of slow and fast times, but the skilled worker is able to produce his fast movements more often. This kind of evidence suggests that an operation may be carried out with varying efficiency by a number of action patterns which differ in detail, so that the acquisition of speed skill consists in learning to recognize and select with increasing *accuracy* from a family of alternative patterns of movement.

PART AND WHOLE METHODS

Another broad question concerns the size and character of the units which give the best return for practice. It is possible to ask whether the learner should practise the whole of a task from the beginning, or whether the task should be broken up into parts which are practised separately. Obviously there is no straightforward answer since the meanings of "whole" and "part" will vary from task to task. However, recommendations of the "whole" method have been prominent in the educational literature.

The two most important factors determining the apparent superiority of whole or part methods appear to be the difficulty of the task and the way in which the part is related to the whole task. The first of these factors, task difficulty, scarcely needs elaboration. The sheer size or complexity of many tasks like aerial photography or weather forecasting makes any recommendation for the whole method of learning impractical. At the same time, as Bugelski (1956) points out, no one would consider the part memorization of small units like a single sentence from a story. Between these two extremes there must be an optimum size of practice unit or, more probably, an optimum range of sizes.

To some extent this optimum size will depend upon the capacity of the individual learner, as O'Brien (1943) found in the memorization of music. Relatively whole methods will tend to favour the more able individuals. No doubt it is for this reason that Clarke and Clarke (1958) recommend part practice for the training of subnormal subjects, since this will tend to present to them the size of unit they can best handle. However, normal subjects also benefit from part practice when the size of the whole exceeds the optimum.

The deterioration in learning efficiency as the size of the practised whole becomes uneconomic is easiest shown in maze-learning, where the task may be readily subdivided into parts. Cook (1937) used a "spider" maze, in which each choice unit presents eight alternatives. These units were combined into groups of two, four, eight and sixteen to make progressively more difficult tasks, which were

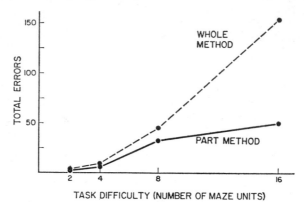

FIG. 25. Increase in errors with "whole" learning as the size of task increases. The error scores represent first learning of the relevant mazes; data on later practice is distorted by other factors. After Cook (1937).

learned either by part or by whole methods. The "part" was in each case half the maze. The information on time and number of trials taken is dubious, since there were several extra trials after each part was learned, but the errors made in learning the maze by both methods are plotted in Fig. 25. Attempting to learn by the whole method generates 200 per cent more errors with the longest maze.

Although part practice becomes more suitable as the size of the task increases, many tasks are not so readily split into parts for separate practice. The second factor which was mentioned as affecting the problem of part or whole learning is this factor of "divisibility". In poetry, for example, where several early experiments favoured whole learning, it might happen that the whole is of an economic size for learning; but alternatively, part practice might be at some disadvantage because it sacrifices some of the contextual information which prompts the learner. Learning line by line would lose the information contributed by the rhyme in traditional poems, and learning stanza by stanza would lose the sequence of ideas which bind the poem together.

In most physical skills the dissection into parts must be approached with even greater caution, the risk being that one has the learner practise a part action which is qualitatively different from its counterpart in the whole activity. Practising the arm movements of the breast-stroke on land may not be the same thing as using them to swim in the water in co-ordination with the legs. In any case the separately learned parts will possibly need subsequent practice to weld them into a whole skill, and this combination stage may need a disproportionate amount of further learning. It is probably these reasons, as much as the optimum difficulty of the unit selected for part practice, which account for the general superiority of the whole method in the several gymnastic skills reviewed by Knapp (1963).

The difficulties in dividing certain skills into parts are seen in a laboratory experiment by Briggs and Brogden (1954). The task involved lever movements in two dimensions, backward–forward and left–right. Separate practice at the backward–forward and the left–right movements was not as efficient as practising the whole task. Learners on the whole task tended to sweep the levers from one point to another in one continuous motion, whereas after part practice the tendency was for them to make separate forward and sideways adjustments. The whole task was well within the learners' capacity, so that the size or difficulty factor may have played a part, but it is undoubtedly important that the whole skill required movements rather different from those involved in part practice.

An experiment by Naylor and Briggs (1963) shows the effects of both factors. In this experiment subjects gave series of guesses, saying whether aircraft carriers or submarines would appear in various zones on a screen and guessing how many would appear. For the whole task subjects had to guess which type of vehicle would appear, how many and where, in a combined prediction. In the part task they guessed the vehicle type or the number or the zone separately. The difficulty of the task was varied by making the sequences of items more, or less, predictable. The part–whole relation was varied in cohesion, by varying the interdependence of the different types of information. Whether a submarine appeared in one of the zones might be quite independent of whether two aircraft carriers appeared in another zone, or the two events might be linked together.

What happened depended upon both of the characteristics of the task, the difficulty and the degree of interdependence. When the parts were independent, the advantage of part training increased as the task became more difficult. This is roughly what we saw in Fig. 25, since we can assume that the parts of the spider maze are independent. However, when the parts were *interdependent* the whole method was superior, especially on the more difficult version of the task. On the surface this seems to present difficulties for anything but whole training on many tasks, since it will very often happen that the parts are interdependent. Fortunately, the rough categories of part and whole do not exhaust the possibilities. There are ways of gradually approaching the whole skill which do not rely upon a brutal fragmentation.

PROGRESSION

In the experiment just described the part training was one of several possible "progression" methods. On the first day subjects practised one part; then on the second day a second part was added and both were practised together; on the third day the third part was added and the whole skill was attained. This is what has been called the "part–continuous" method by Barton (1921), who showed its advantage compared with the whole learning of mazes. Part–continuous training represents one of several attempts at overcoming the learner's difficulty in recombining separated parts.

Another variant of this technique, "progressive–part" training, is advocated by Seymour (1954). If a cycle of work on a capstan lathe requires four operations—loading, cross slide operation, turret operation and unloading—these may be practised separately. When the operator can do these at a target speed the first and second, like the third and fourth operations, can be practised as pairs. Following this, operations one, two and three, and operations two, three and four are practised as groups until a given level of proficiency is reached; the operator is finally transferred to whole practice, in which all four operations are carried out as a single sequence.

Seymour (1956) compared the whole method with progressive–part training and with a straightforward part or "isolation" method. The part methods were better than whole training (Fig. 26). However, plain part training and the progressive–part method appeared equally good, just as Barton (1921) had found. The analysis which Cook (1937) made of part maze-learning showed that the errors made when learners had to combine the parts which they practised separately were very few, and contributed little to the total number of errors made during learning. It seems therefore that if a task can be meaningfully subdivided, reconstituting the task from its parts will cause no difficulty. We may tentatively conclude that the continuous and progression methods of part practice have little to offer.

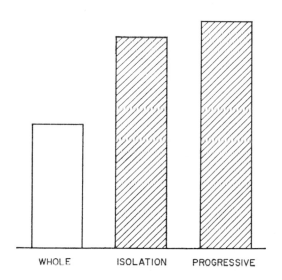

WHOLE   ISOLATION   PROGRESSIVE

FIG. 26. Errorless runs on a capstan lathe after three kinds of training. After Seymour (1956).

What all part methods have to contribute is the opportunity to concentrate practice upon the difficult segments of a skill, and a kind of motivational bonus due to the readier evidence of progress provided by mastering any part. The part learner obtains earlier satisfaction from his achievements and can often make more direct use of knowledge of results. A similar high ratio of satisfaction can be obtained with a different kind of progressive practice—the "gradual metamorphosis" method. Just as a child's first attempts at making marks on paper gradually change into the ability to make straight lines or circles, through practice which is not really on the whole skill or any part of it, the attempts of adult learners can be gradually transformed into what is required.

In this kind of training the learner is led by short imperceptible steps from what he can do to what he should do, just as the "behaviour shaping" mentioned in an earlier chapter proceeds by successive approximation. In verbal learning this kind of technique is embodied in the "programming" of information into a consecutive series of small items, so that the student is finally equipped to do, say trigonometry, without ever practising the whole task. Teaching machines, which are discussed later, work in this way.

Gradual progression of this kind has been little analysed in human physical skills, although it is implicit in many training procedures and seems an important alternative to the "whole" method. For example, it seems possible and extremely efficient to progress by gradual stages from the performance of a forward roll to carrying out headsprings and handsprings in the gymnasium (Whiteley, 1963). At first, the forward roll is carried out on a platform at ground level. Next the platform is gradually raised, with practice at each new level, and then made narrower, so that the learner becomes accustomed to landing on his feet. Finally the platform is again gradually lowered, so that more weight is taken on the arms and the roll has become a handspring. One advantage of this technique in gymnastics is that the learner's anxiety is never aroused, since he is never asked to outstrip his current ability. There seems to be no reason why many other skills should not be similarly programmed and no doubt experimental evidence will soon appear.

MASSED AND SPACED PRACTICE

Learning archery by shooting one arrow every year is likely to be an inefficient training schedule, and so is attempting to learn heraldry at a single sitting. Within these extremes there is a broad range of spacings of practice which will make very little difference to what is eventually learned. However, the problem is not as simple as it appears since a large number of factors will influence the outcome of any particular experiment on the distribution of practice. These are probably best appreciated in the context of a specific example.

In an experiment on juggling with three balls Knapp and Dixon (1950) found that a group of senior students who learned for five minutes every day spent less time in actual practice than a group which learned for fifteen minutes every other day. The first problem is to decide which group had massed practice. The authors assume that the fifteen-minute group was massed, and the five-minute group spaced. However, the rest interval between fifteen-minute sessions was a day longer than the rest between the five-minute sessions, which suggests the reverse. On the other hand the fifteen-minute group did have a longer work period and is thus relatively massed; but within the work periods both groups had continuous, not spaced, practice. The problem, then, is that spacing may vary separately between practice sessions, between trials or runs or lists in these sessions, and often between responses as well.

A second kind of problem concerns the measure of efficiency. Although the practice time was shorter for the five-minute group they had to come for practice on thirteen occasions, against eight for the five-minute group. Alternatively, if the resting periods are considered part of the total learning time the fifteen-minute group had not learned until fifteen days had elapsed. Further, since only accuracy was measured there might be a hidden difference in speed of performance between the two groups.

A third problem area, of greater theoretical interest, requires investigation rather than definition. Did the fifteen-minute group become fatigued or muddled during practice? Did their level of skill therefore improve between practice sessions, rather than during practice, as the effects of protracted concentration wore off? Did they rehearse during the rest interval? What would have happened if the fifteen minutes had been split into three sets of five minutes by rest pauses of five minutes, or one minute, or one hour? Did they need time to "warm up" after two days' rest? What would have happened if the two groups had been tested again the following week? Naturally enough these questions have attracted a great deal of experimental attention; a recent review (Bilodeau and Bilodeau, 1961) lists over fifty relevant papers on motor skills, while verbal learning (Underwood, 1961) undoubtedly accounts for a similar number. Owing to the variety of possible experimental designs and measures many points of detail remain obscure, although the broad outlines seem reasonably clear.

Much of what typically happens is illustrated in Fig. 27, which gives the results of an experiment by Digman (1959). The task was to keep a stylus in contact with a target revolving "epicyclically"— circles within circles. The "spaced" or "distributed" group rested for one and a half minutes between half-minute practice trials, while the

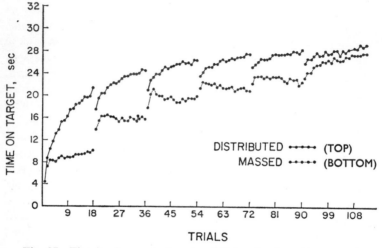

TRIALS

Fig. 27. The development of motor skill by distributed or massed practice. From Digman (1959).

"massed" group had a break of only two seconds. Each group had eighteen trials a day; and the breaks in the graph separate their performance on the six days of practice.

On the first day—the first section on the graph—the typical effect of massed practice appears. Compared with the distributed group the massed subjects show little apparent improvement. However, their performance has been artificially depressed by the massing and is not a true indication of learning. On the second day they begin higher than they left off, having apparently learned overnight. This is the phenomenon known technically as "reminiscence", in defiance of the usual meaning of the word, and is presumably due to their recovery from a kind of psychological fatigue. We see next that the distributed group, on the second and each subsequent day, begins lower than at the end of the previous day; some "warm-up" is needed, but improvement throughout each day is continuous. By contrast the massed group appears to deteriorate throughout each day of practice up to the fifth, except for the brief initial rise we have attributed to "warm-up"; their gains are made *between* the practice sessions. On the last day, the massed group too is given spaced trials and *the difference between the two groups nearly disappears.*

RESIDUAL EFFECTS

Had the final practice session been massed the difference between massed and spaced groups would still have almost disappeared. Using well over two thousand subjects Reynolds and Adams (1953) transferred groups from massed to spaced practice, and from spaced to massed practice, after varying numbers of trials. In each case the transferring group soon approached the level of performance appropriate to their new conditions of practice, and there was scant evidence for any permanent disadvantage due to massing. Sometimes a slight difference does remain; Jahnke and Duncan (1956) found some differences between massed and spaced groups after an interval of four weeks. In these cases it is important to discover the reason for the discrepancy.

In the first place, the distributed groups may gain some benefit from mental rehearsal during rest pauses. As we shall see, mental practice is tolerably efficient; and sometimes when the rest pause is filled with an activity like watching coloured slides, which would prevent mental rehearsal, there is no residual advantage in spaced practice (Shucker, Stevens and Ellis, 1953). Of equal importance is the idea that massed and spaced groups do not necessarily get the same amounts of real practice. Equal practice is not assured merely by allotting the same amount of practice time to both groups, since they may not both be able to make full use of the time. The performance of the massed groups is often depressed by fatigue, which may mean that they do measurably less work during practice.

Differences in the use of practice time are easily shown in a task where separate responses may be identified and counted. Printing letters of the alphabet upside down, a task often used in this field, is slowed down by massing of the work period; and Archer (1954) has shown that making allowance for the number of letters printed reveals somewhat better learning by the massed subjects.

Similarly, in two of three tasks studied by Reynolds and Bilodeau (1952), it was possible to equate efficiency, rather than time spent, in practice. In "complex co-ordination" massed and spaced subjects

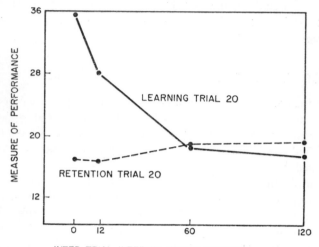

FIG. 28. Recovery after rest from the effects of massed practice. The lower the performance score, the better the performance. By the 20th trial of original learning the massed groups, with shorter rests between trials, are at an apparent disadvantage. The retention trials ten weeks later show that all groups have reached about the same level of performance. After Reynolds and Bilodeau (1952).

made the same number of position settings of red to green lights; in the "pursuit rotor" test both groups spent the same amount of time with the stylus on target. Despite the usual early differences during training no permanent effects of massing remained in a test ten weeks later (Fig. 28).

To the extent that any residual effects of massing are due to differences in the quality of practice during the allotted time, it is clearly vital to pay attention to the detailed course of events during learning. Changing the gross time intervals may have little effect—Franklin and Brozek (1947) found no differences between spells of practice once, twice or three times a day—and the results of manipulating hours and weeks probably depend upon what occurs during the minutes and seconds of ongoing practice.

In the inverted alphabet printing task Archer and Bourne (1956) noticed that the increased time under massed practice was due to lingering between letters, while the time taken to write the letters remained constant. The implication is that subjects were spacing their own practice by resting between responses. Sustained concentration is impossible in any demanding task (Broadbent, 1958a). If frequent rest pauses are not available the subject will involuntarily make his own; the eyes will blink, the attention will waver and in a paced task like the pursuit rotor the result will be a poorer score. In some cases the lapses in attention will accumulate to produce an appreciable deficit in real learning time and there will be some permanent advantage for the spaced groups. This will usually be small since mainly the early, unfamiliar stages of practice will be affected; depriving people of incoming information later in practice has relatively little effect.

Lapses in attention in verbal learning seem less important than muddles between similar responses, if indeed the two effects are separate. In either case one might suppose that the usual procedure of presenting the words in a list to be learned one at a time, or a pair at a time, provides ample momentary rest pauses. It does appear generally that even the immediate effects of massing tend to be smaller in verbal learning. However, Hovland (1938) showed that extending the time interval between items from two to four seconds is more important than the degree of massing or spacing represented by six seconds or two minutes longer, between lists. Again we may note the importance of small-scale time effects.

As a general rule we may conclude that some practice will be inefficient if the learner is asked to concentrate for too long without a break. Of course, this is not a universal recommendation that learning should be spaced as widely as possible; although erring on the side of spacing can do little harm other than wasting time, unless the breaks are so long that appreciable forgetting occurs.

MENTAL PRACTICE

In verbal learning we are well accustomed to the notion of mental practice. Silently rehearsing a poem, or list of items, is not thought untoward. Practising gymnastic or other bodily skills in this way is less widely accepted, although there are good reasons for recommending its use. The advantages of practice are not due merely to the fact that a number of perceptual events have been followed by responses and their consequences. In order to affect the learner's behaviour these events must have modified the internal connections of the brain. Obviously, if we could modify the brain of the learner directly we could dispense with physical practice sessions altogether, provided that we could predict the results of his potential actions with sufficient exactness.

We cannot in fact put in a scalpel and stir up new learning, but we can arrange for "internal practice" which will programme the brain of the learner by juxtaposing internal stimuli and internal

Fig. 29. Muscle record from a person instructed to imagine hitting a nail twice with a hammer. From Jacobson (1932).

responses. The notion of such internal events may seem a little dubious, but descriptions need not be logically respectable in order to convey information. We do know that measurable nerve activity occurs on the output side of the organism when no apparent action is taking place, so that "internal responses" do exist. Jacobson (1932) measured the incipient responses of arm muscles when people were asked to imagine that they were carrying out various activities, like climbing a rope or rowing a boat. Figure 29 shows the record of a subject imagining a rhythmical activity, hitting twice with a hammer.

On the input side there is also good reason to talk, however guardedly, of internal events. Internal stimuli often appear as imagery, not necessarily of course as visual imagery, although the term tends to suggest mental pictures. This is where Sackett (1934) began. At that time there was considerable interest in maze-learning, and it was believed that people tended to remember the path through finger mazes in one of three main ways.

In Sackett's case about 25 per cent seemed to use verbal imagery, remembering "right, left, left, right, left" and so on; another 10 per cent used a kind of motor imagery, while the 65 per cent majority depended upon visual imagery. Sackett thought it useful to exploit these processes by requiring subjects to practise mentally for a week. Since visual imagery seemed common, he also included a group who practised drawing diagrams of the maze. The drawing group and the mental practice group did improve substantially during the week. However, a non-practising group, included for control purposes, also improved a great deal and the demonstration is not satisfactory.

One might expect better results with an adjustive skill; and a carefully designed series of experiments by Vandell, Davis and Clugston (1943) confirms this impression. They investigated dart-throwing and basketball-aiming by children of different ages and college students, matched for each comparison in terms of age, sex and intelligence. With older children and students physical and mental practice appeared to reach the same limit of improvement. Younger children were better after mental practice than a control group, although in their case physical practice gave greater improvement, possibly because they had not had sufficient experience of the real task before the experiment began.

A number of other investigators have studied the effects of mental practice, with favourable results. Perry (1939) tried five tasks—card sorting, a pegboard exercise, number substitution, controlled tapping and mirror drawing. In piano playing (Rubin-Rabson, 1941) mental practice appeared best placed in the middle stages of learning. Twining (1949) compared quarter of an hour's daily mental practice at ring-tossing with the effects of spending the same time making seventy actual throws on to a peg. Steel (1952) used the throwing of tennis balls at a target.

The "Pacific Coast one hand foul shot", which is a kind of basketball throw, was evaluated by Clark (1960) with three different classes of performer. Again there was an indication that the mental practice of novices was hampered by their lack of prior experience. According to Klausmeier (1962) Waterland tried tenpin bowling, finding that concentration upon a smooth flowing movement pattern was desirable. Kelsey (1961) found a tendency for mental practice to improve muscular endurance.

In nearly every case mental practice is somewhat inferior to direct physical practice, but appreciably better than no practice. Clearly, it could form a valuable supplement to many schemes of training. The reason why it is not more commonly adopted is probably the obscureness of the activity, and its inaccessibility to external control. Even in universities those in authority are reluctant to schedule time for students merely to sit and think. In an industrial training scheme mental practice is best encouraged outside working hours, since "I was practising mentally" may not always be sympathetically received.

SUMMARY

Skills are built up by practice, which allows the learner to form associations between stimuli and responses. Associations between one set of stimulus conditions and the next allow him to anticipate the course of events, making his performance smoother and more predictable. Improvement slackens off as skill is attained, giving rise to the typical learning curve. The way in which learning progresses is affected by the conditions in which the task is practised.

Speed and accuracy. The distinction between learning to practise fast and learning to practise accurately is often artificial. Any differences between the two procedures are likely to hinge upon whether or not changing the speed of performance materially affects the nature of the practised task. At least in a repetitive task speed of performance seems to depend upon the accuracy with which the learner monitors his own activities.

Part and whole. As the size or complexity of a task increases it becomes inefficient for the beginner to tackle the whole task. Discrete, repetitive or serial tasks are easily subdivided into parts which may then be practised separately. Tasks requiring continuous adjustment, or in which for various reasons the parts are interdependent, suffer by subdivision into parts.

Despite the absence of formal evidence, the best solution here seems to be a form of *gradual progression* in which simpler skills are slowly transformed into more demanding activities. The units in early practice of this kind are therefore *small wholes* rather than *parts*.

Massing and spacing. A number of complicating factors enter into most studies of massed and spaced practice. When these factors are carefully controlled it is clear that the effects of massed practice are almost entirely confined to depressing the immediate performance of a task, with little detriment to the eventual level of learning. *Massed* groups, practising for long periods with at most short rest pauses, often appear temporarily inferior to *spaced* groups who practise for short periods with relatively long rest pauses. Giving a complete rest, or placing both groups on massed or on spaced schedules, tends to equalize the performance levels.

Any differences which remain are probably due (1) to the tendency of massed groups to do less practice, or to attend less consecutively to what they do practise, and (2) to the opportunity afforded to spaced groups for consolidating their learning by mental practice.

Mental practice. All the evidence suggests that mental practice works, although not of course as well as direct physical practice. Encouraging learners to "go over things in their heads" is probably a valuable addition to training.

7. TRANSFER OF TRAINING

LEARNING one task affects one's learning of the next. The more similar the two tasks are, the more interaction there will be between them. To some extent eating with chopsticks resembles handling tweezers, so that a habitual stamp collector will be affected by the tweezer habit in his learning of chopstick mastery. The relationship between the two tasks may be investigated from either end: if we are interested in the effect of stamp collecting on chopstick handling, we are concerned with *transfer of training*; if we are instead interested in the effect which using chopsticks has upon the earlier learned manipulation of tweezers, we are concerned with *retroaction*. Both transfer and retroaction effects may either facilitate or hinder the learning of the other task. In order to know which will happen we must examine both the perceptual and motor relations between the tasks, in terms of the previous experience of the learner.

SAMENESS AND DIFFERENCE

Transfer of learning occurs throughout the life of an individual. All adult learning depends partly upon the transfer of previously learned habits and methods of approach, since all learning situations have some characteristics in common. For the individual learner, the similarities between situations change progressively in several ways.

At any given moment there will be a tendency to react in the same way to a range of physically different stimuli. In terms of behaviour, a range of colours or tones or smells may all be functionally equivalent. If we teach a child to open his mouth for chocolate when we touch his hand, touching his wrist or elbow will tend to evoke the same reaction; the touch stimulus is *generalized*. This is really transfer of training on a small scale. Figure 30 shows the curves obtained by first training people to press a key on hearing a musical tone, and then observing how often they pressed the key in response to higher or lower notes, or to louder and softer notes.

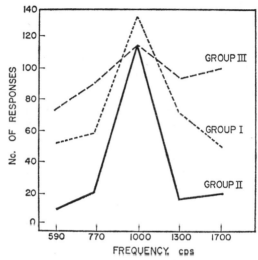

FIG. 30. The spread of similarity. The groups were all tested at different pitches after training on 1000 cps. Group II always had the same note during training, while groups I and III had experience of different loudnesses. From Hoving (1963)

Throughout life finer discriminations and wider generalizations develop. If we find that reacting to a sound of a certain pitch brings one result, while reacting in the same way to a similar note brings another, we come to discriminate between the two in our behaviour. Part of the psychological equipment of a person skilled in any activity is the ability to make perceptual distinctions which are too fine for the novice to distinguish. A pigeon fancier can readily tell the sex of his birds—the males have larger heads—although like the Chinese, they all look alike to the newcomer. The limits of similarity are set closer for the expert.

At the same time, we have to learn to group together apparently disparate objects. A "Granny Smith" is hard, shiny and green, while a russet is soggy, wrinkled and brown, but both must be recognized as apples and treated alike in the appropriate circumstances. For human beings, words play an important part in helping this process of grouping and classifying. We readily learn a word like "money" which associates for us physical objects as different as coins and banknotes. Of course, words themselves acquire sameness; in fact we are more likely to treat "road" and "path" in the same way, although "road" and "rowed" are physically more similar (Razran, 1940).

These fluctuating samenesses and differences are altered by training, and themselves affect the way in which transfer takes place. Regular training on a given task allows us to isolate relevant groups of stimuli and, through mechanisms like knowledge of results, gradually strengthens our tendency to respond consistently to them in certain ways. If we are then transferred to a similar task, our training transfers. Naturally enough, to the extent that the stimulus conditions are similar we tend to react in a similar way. If the same movements are needed, we are equipped to produce them in different surroundings. How valuable these tendencies are in the second task will depend upon whether or not similar responses are appropriate.

RELATIONS BETWEEN TASKS

In many everyday activities it is not easy to decide how similar the perceptual and motor aspects of the two tasks are. The similarities and differences between cricket and baseball are too complicated for analysis in advance, and only direct observation will tell us whether learning one hinders or helps learning the other. In the laboratory it is possible to investigate simplified situations in which the relations between tasks may be specified fairly exactly.

The theoretical position resulting from the early work (Poffenberger, 1915; Wylie, 1919; Bruce, 1933) is summed up in a simplified form in Table 3. This shows the transfer effects to be expected when perceptual similarity and the similarity of the necessary responses are varied separately. These relationships have been laid out by Osgood (1949) in a way which attempts to allow for different degrees of similarity, and many of his predictions have been verified in the learning of pairs of words by Bugelski and Cadwallader (1956) and Dallett (1962).

The first case illustrated by the table is simple. Obviously, if both tasks present the same stimuli and require the same responses, the tasks are identical and no transfer problem exists. If we have learned to press a button in response to a red light, pressing the button the next time the red light appears is merely a continuation of the same learning process. The second case, where both stimuli and responses are different, again requires little discussion. If both tasks are different no problem, and no transfer, should arise. This condition is not always easy to arrange, since remote or abstract similarities are hard to exclude.

TABLE 3. Transfer between tasks depends on both
perceptual and response similarity

	Task Stimuli	Response Required	Transfer
1	Same	Same	High
2	Different	Different	None
3	Different	Same	Positive
4	Same	Different (but similar)	Negative (?)

The third case considers what transfer occurs when different stimuli are presented but the same response is required. Here we can readily generalize our previous learning from one stimulus context to another. The case where both sets of stimuli are the same shades gradually into the case where both are less similar or completely different. Instead of the red light we can respond to an orange one, or a green one, or even to a bell or a pistol shot. The effects of previous practice on the motor side of the task, which includes, of course, the perceptual data directly bearing upon the execution of the response, give the same kind of benefit when the same response is repeated in a new context. Since the new task is begun with some advantage due to learning the first task, we say that transfer is *positive*.

We can turn the procedure round and test how performance on the first task has been affected by learning the second. With the same response required to different stimuli, the first task will probably have benefited—an example of "retroactive facilitation".

Both transfer and retroactive effects may be adverse in some cases. Had learning the first task made people worse on the second task than they would otherwise have been, transfer would be *negative*; and the parallel effect in reverse is "retroactive interference".

An experiment by Singleton (1957) in which the first task was a non-laboratory, industrial skill, helps to make clear the relationships so far considered. A group of sewing-machine operators with twenty years' experience were tested alongside a control group with no previous training, on a task which reproduced some features of boot-and-shoe stitching. One of the relevant industrial operations is the production of short rows of exact numbers of stitches. These were represented by a row of neon bulbs which flashed on successively at speeds from 2300 lights per minute. The comparable experimental task to which transfer from previous experience was measured consisted of attempting to light an exact number of bulbs by various methods. The operator might press and release a morse key by hand or by foot, or use a standard sewing machine treadle.

Using the morse key to operate the lights is different in both its stimulus and its reponse aspects from the original sewing experience. There were no differences between the skilled and inexperienced groups in this part of the experiment; hence no transfer had occurred from the previous sewing experience. On the other hand, the previously skilled group did have an advantage in controlling the lights by means of the foot treadle. This was an example of the different stimulus–same response category, and thus showed positive transfer.

One combination was not explored: operators might have been presented with shoe seams (same stimuli) and asked to sew them with morse keys (different response). The combination of same stimuli and different response, as the table indicates, might have resulted in negative transfer. That is to say, the skilled operators might have been at a disadvantage on the new task. However, it is also possible that no transfer might take place, or that after some initial readjustment previous training might prove a positive advantage.

One case of the same stimuli with apparently different responses is that of "bilateral transfer", where training is transferred from the left hand to the right hand, or from arm to leg. These combinations usually give successful results because, of course, effectively the same response is required although it is carried out with different parts of the body. Cook (1934) plotted out the transfer relations between hands and feet quite systematically, showing that transfer was greater between symmetrical members and least diagonally between hand and foot. Bilateral transfer is not really a problem to fit into our table of relationships, but unfortunately one often finds other examples of the same stimulus–different response category which also yield positive transfer, so that the case of negative transfer requires more analysis.

NEGATIVE TRANSFER

If we practise a given response to certain stimuli, we will tend to produce the same response the next time we are in that situation. If a different response is now required, the old response is inappropriate and the result should be negative transfer. Of course the two situations cannot be absolutely identical or there would be no means of knowing that a different response is required. Sometimes the key stimuli which constitute the "instruction" to perform one or other response are present all the time, and making the new response is not difficult; if we are presented with a bow and arrow instead of a rifle it will not be difficult to overcome the tendency to press a non-existent trigger at the sight of a target. At other times the key or instructions have to be borne in mind, and lapses may occur. If we have learned to press "F" on the piano to a blob in the lower space of staff music, it is not always easy to remember a "sharp" at the beginning of the page and to press the black note above "F" instead.

What happens, then, is that muddles tend to occur over which response is appropriate. On the whole this is unlikely when the old and new responses are easily discriminable (Gagné, Baker and Foster, 1956). The theoretical position over negative transfer is still unsatisfactory, but the accumulated evidence suggests that muddles are particularly likely when responses are highly similar in the two tasks, but differ in small but important ways. In motor learning this typically happens when movements of the same extent, duration and force are made to the left in the first task and to the right in the second, or when the difference between upward and downward movement is all that matters (Adams, 1954).

Another situation in which confusion is easy occurs when the task is composed of a number of stimulus–response pairs and these are re-paired for the second task. The responses for the second task as a whole are now identical with those of the first, but differ in the order in which they are required. After learning to respond with the word "crafty" to the stimulus "equal", then "humid" to "noble" and "healthy" to "stony", we might next be required to give "angry", "yellow" and "sudden" in response to the original "equal", "noble" and "stony". These are completely different responses for the same stimuli. Alternatively we might be faced with the stimulus-response pairs: "equal–humid", "noble–healthy" and "stony–crafty"; these are the original words in a new combination. Comparing these two kinds of task, Porter and Duncan (1953) found positive transfer to the completely different verbal responses but negative transfer to those occurring in a new pairing.

Loosely, then, we expect more negative transfer the more similar are the responses required in the two tasks. The same effect was observed in early work on retroactive interference, and was formulated as the Skaggs–Robinson hypothesis (Skaggs, 1925; Robinson, 1927). As the originally learned material and the subsequent material cease to be identical the "retroactive" effect on re-testing the original material quickly reaches a maximum; this happens because the experimenter distinguishes the two sets of material but the subject does not (Ritchie, 1954). As the two materials increase in difference, the subject generalizes less across the two situations and less interference takes place (Fig. 31).

It is for this sort of reason that schools prefer to teach hockey with association football during the same season. Association and rugby football are too close for comfort; so are Spanish and Portuguese, whereas language departments have less qualms over the combination of Spanish with French. For similar reasons, it pays to evaluate very carefully the efficiency for the real task of training on an artificial simulator (Lawrence, 1954). Simulators, like gunnery or driving instruction models, often differ slightly from the task they simulate; as before, if the differences are important there may be negative transfer. Retraining for new industrial tasks may sometimes present a problem, too. Entwisle (1959) showed some delays in re-learning, and a tendency to have more accidents, in drivers changing from horse-drawn to motor vehicles.

However, negative effects are often confined to the early stages of the new learning, and even here are often represented as sporadic wrong responses rather than an overall depression of performance. How important this is in practice will depend upon the nature of the task and the seriousness of an error. If we practise giving change with our left hand we shall obtain positive bilateral transfer for the manipulation of money, and the fact that we occasionally dip into the wrong pocket will be unimportant. On the other hand,

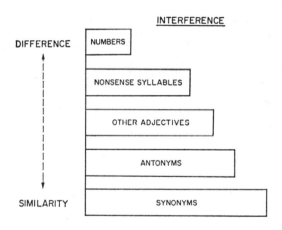

FIG. 31. Decrease in interference as the lists of interpolated words are made less similar to those originally learned. Based on the percentage forgotten over and above the loss during rest. After McGeoch and McDonald (1931).

if a pilot risks making a single interfering response near the ground, such as kicking the rudder in the opposite direction to the joystick with a resulting sideslip, the possibility of a crash enhances the importance of even slight tendencies towards negative transfer. For many skills, where a modicum of early errors is acceptable, attempting to predict negative transfer is largely of academic interest.

LONG-TERM EFFECTS

Since tasks which produce interference are closely similar in many ways there is also a great deal of positive transfer between the two. Positive and negative effects may cancel out, or one or other tendency may dominate during the early stages. In certain kinds of experiment it is possible to measure both effects simultaneously; a matching task used by Lewis, McAllister and Adams (1951) showed increases in both number of correct responses and number of errors. McFann (1953) demonstrated both effects in a tracing task.

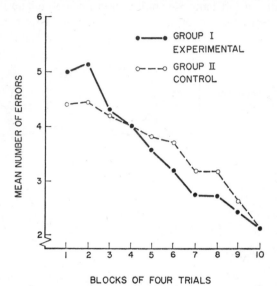

FIG. 32. Negative transfer changing first to positive and later to zero transfer. The experimental group, transferring from verbal pre-training, begins with more errors than the control group; during the second half of the curve the control group makes more errors; both groups finish with the same score. From McCormack (1958).

Thus at various stages of learning the second task overall positive or negative transfer may appear, depending both upon the weighting given to errors and upon whether one's ability to perform a similar response has outstripped one's discrimination between the old and the new situations. An example may be taken from the work on verbal pre-training, where it was pointed out that verbal and motor responses to the same stimuli might interfere with one another. In McCormack's (1958) experiment (Fig. 32), initially negative transfer gives way to positive transfer while, as often happens, by the end of the experiment both groups are performing equally well.

In other cases negative transfer may not appear until some

practice has taken place on the second task. In Adams' (1954) experiment, for instance, reversing the display–control relationships did not produce negative transfer effects until after six or seven trials at the second task. Many people are familiar with this effect in driving a car abroad. By and large there is positive transfer from driving on the left to driving on the right. Compared with a novice a skilled driver does very well in another country, with the sole but unfortunate exception of the odd intrusive error which may occur after several days of successful driving on the opposite side from usual. In such cases one tends to assume that initial positive transfer was shored up by self-instructions which lapse after the initial anxieties are lulled.

The driving example prompts another observation; interference may be worse on changing back to the old task. Returning to driving on the left after a spell of driving on the right may be more confusing than the original change. This, too, may be found in an experimental setting. Deese and Hardman (1954) showed greater retroactive interference than negative transfer between the same two verbal tasks. Their explanation is in terms of the amount of learning on the task from which the change took place, and again it appears generally true that the stage of learning reached on the prior task is crucial.

It has long been clear that if two tasks are favourably related, the greater the learning on the prior task the greater will be the positive transfer. On the other hand, there is also evidence that *interference* between tasks will be greatest when the prior learning is at an intermediate stage. Mandler (1954), for instance, showed this in a motor task, as did Bugelski (1942) for verbal learning. As first task learning increases negative transfer first increases also, but then diminishes as one's perceptual grasp of the task's distinguishing characteristics grows, so that a well-learned task tends to interfere relatively little with a following similar task.

It seems likely that one's tendency to generalize from the task stimuli to other similar stimuli often increases early in practice (Gagné and Foster, 1949); if this occurs with both first and second tasks maximum interference will take place at this stage, when both tasks are maximally "confusable". In fact, Siipola and Israel (1933) did find most interference when both first and second tasks were at an intermediate stage of learning, but the number of factors involved in transfer makes such a conclusion appear deceptively simple.

One way of improving perceptual discrimination is repeatedly to compare similar examples. Thus it is not surprising to find that repeatedly changing to and from interfering tasks quickly abolishes negative transfer and that positive advantages may supervene (Lewis, McAllister and Bechtoldt, 1953). Such training produces a flexibility of performance which may often be of use, and Wolfle (1951) goes so far as to suggest that providing a variety of practice materials is one of the main principles of training. Some confirmation is provided by Duncan (1958), who compared the effects of training on 1, 2, 5 or 10 versions of a lights-and-lever task. He showed that the more varied training methods give greater transfer even when the stimulus lights are replaced by nonsense syllables.

TASK DIFFICULTY

When two tasks differ in difficulty it is often found that transfer between them is unequal. Let us suppose that playing the organ is more difficult than playing the piano. We might find that learning to play the organ gives more transfer to learning the piano than learning the piano does to playing the organ; there has been greater transfer in the difficult–easy direction than in the easy–difficult direction.

A word of caution is probably needed here, since people have sometimes assumed that the direction of greater transfer is the direction which training should take. This does not really follow, since if all we want is to play the piano we shall probably be better off practising the piano from the start. The fact that there might be less transfer to the organ, and more transfer from the organ, is curious but irrelevant to our purpose. Admittedly, it has occasionally been found that practising another version of the task gives better results than practising the task itself, but this is a separate issue which has already arisen in one form in our discussion of the part–whole problem. To labour the point further, let us assume that transfer to piano-playing from previous practice of piano-playing represents 100 per cent, that transfer from organ to piano is 80 per cent and transfer from piano to organ is 50 per cent. There is more transfer from organ to piano than in the reverse direction, but neither is as efficient as playing the piano. It is mainly when we wish to perform a series of tasks, rather than a single task, that the order in which they are learned takes on practical importance.

An early example of unequal transfer was provided by Szafran and Welford (1950), who taught groups of subjects to throw chains at a target under three conditions. The easiest version was direct throwing. Throwing the chains over a bar was intermediate, while throwing indirectly and using a mirror to see the obscured target was most difficult. When subjects were transferred from the version upon which they had practised to one of the other forms of the task, it appeared that transfer was higher from the difficult to the easy version than in the reverse direction.

Baker, Wylie and Gagné (1950) varied the gear ratio in a tracking task, so that subjects had to move faster to follow the target at each of its speeds, with results again favouring difficult-to-easy transfer. Similar findings were indicated when Gibbs (1951) varied the complexity of a tracking task; and it began to appear that difficulty was an important factor in predicting transfer of training.

However, opposing results soon appeared. Where a difficult discrimination is to be built up, as in comparing sounds of different pitch (Baker and Osgood, 1954), transferring from an easier version seems better than training on the difficult task itself. In motor skills, changes of target speed always tend to transfer better from the slower, easier speeds (Lincoln and Smith, 1951; Ammons, Ammons and Morgan, 1956; Lordahl and Archer, 1958). If people practise reacting quickly to a single stimulus, their later performance with a choice of stimuli improves, unlike the simple reaction times for persons trained on the more difficult choice task (Poulton, 1956); this again favours transfer in the easy–difficult direction. Clearly, then, there is no question of assuming that transfer from the difficult to the easy is universally superior, nor that the idea of difficulty is of any use in helping us to predict what transfer will take place.

In fact, there is no such thing as "difficulty". For convenience we call tasks "difficult" which show a high error score or a long learning curve, but these effects are obtained by varying quite specific characteristics of the task like speed or target size or number of choices. These task characteristics will make their own special demands upon the subject and will lead to quite different transfer effects, regardless of whether or not they happen to produce the same error score. We must thus attempt to group these differing task characteristics in terms of principles which make sense of the unequal transfer they produce.

E

It has been suggested (Day, 1956) that studies in which variation of the motor elements of the task predominate are those which tend to show better transfer in the difficult–easy direction, while those in which the difficulty depends upon one's perceptual grasp of what is needed do not. There is an element of truth in this, but it is certainly not the whole truth. It is difficult to accept the interposing of a mirror between the thrower and his target as a mainly motor change, in order to predict a difficult-to-easy superiority; and it is equally difficult to accept changes in tracking speed as a mainly perceptual problem, to predict the reverse. Two other principles or groups of principles are therefore proposed, which partially overlap the perceptual–motor distinction.

The first is that of *inclusion*. Many tasks in some sense include their easier versions, so that after practising to shoot at an apple, no further practice is needed to hit a barn door; again, if one receives Morse at twenty-four words a minute, there is no difficulty in dropping the rate to eighteen. Usually the easy task does not include the difficult in this way, and inclusion will therefore tend to favour difficult-to-easy transfer. Inclusion will be present often, but not exclusively, in cases where variation of the motor elements is primary, as in changing from heavy to lightweight lifting.

Opposing the influence on transfer of inclusion will be a group of tendencies which may be loosely grouped as *performance standards*. If practice on an easy task gives rise to errors of small size, and if these standards are carried over to a more difficult version where an error of the same real size is proportionately smaller, there will be greater transfer in changing *to* the difficult version than in changing *from* the difficult version. On the difficult version looser standards of performance will have become customary, and carrying these over to the easier task will result in a poor error score. Further, subjects learning the easier version of some skills may acquire tendencies to prefer accuracy over speed, which will raise their standards of performance in the more difficult task. Transfer effects for any given task characteristic will thus depend upon the outcome which is favoured in the balance between inclusion and performance standards—in a sense, the balance between the amount which is learned and how well it is learned.

In a tracking task it is possible to vary the amplitude, or width of movement of the target, and the number of wobbles, or frequencies, in the target course. Holding (1962) used both these characteristics to explore the effects of inclusion and performance standards. Constructing easy courses with few frequencies, and adding in extra frequencies to make more complicated target courses, led to uniform

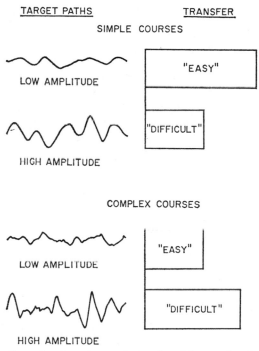

FIG. 33. Opposing transfer results produced by two levels of complexity in a tracking task. More transfer from easy to difficult versions of a simple course, and more transfer from difficult to easy versions of a complex course. After Holding (1962).

superiority of transfer in the difficult–easy direction. Here we may assume that there was straightforward inclusion of the simple courses in the more difficult ones.

However, in a second experiment both effects were observed. When we vary difficulty by changing the amplitude of the target motion, the best direction of transfer will depend upon the degree of complication, or number of frequencies, in the target course. In a simple course changing from a small, easy amplitude to a large, difficult amplitude will give full scope to the transfer of good performance standards from the easier course, and better easy-to-difficult transfer is obtained (Fig. 33). With more complex courses it is no longer possible to keep standards intact when transferring to the higher amplitude course, and the opposite result—better difficult-to-easy transfer—appears as a result of inclusion.

TRANSFER OF PRINCIPLES

Performance standards are not responses. The earlier exposition of transfer in terms of similar or different stimuli and responses must now be modified, to take account of the hypotheses, methods and principles which seem to assist in the transfer of human, and animal, learning. However, it is not always easy to decide exactly what the relevant experiments demonstrate. In Knight's (1924) experiment, for instance, pupils were taught the addition of fractions using as denominators either all numbers up to 30 or only the even numbers. This second group learned the principles of addition efficiently, and transferred perfectly to the task of using the complete range of denominators.

While this experiment has been put forward as an example of the transfer of principles, it is not difficult to see the experimental group as using series of similar responses to cope with similar stimuli. Nevertheless, quite abstract characteristics of responses, such as speed habits, do transfer. No one describes these as "principles", presumably because they are not accompanied by a verbal formulation.

Transfer of principles is usually invoked in experiments of the problem-solving kind. Katona's (1940) work with series of card tricks and matchstick problems shows that there are learning differences between subjects who extract general similarities of method and those who attend to the detailed characteristics of a series of examples. Sometimes formulating the procedure for one trick will help in solving another. Of course, abstracting principles from examples can as readily lead to negative transfer, as Luchins (1942) has shown. If subjects solve a series of problems requiring three operations, like measuring 5 quarts when given jars holding 18, 43 and 10 quarts, they tend to use the same methods in solving simpler problems. Thus, when given jars holding 23, 49 and 3 quarts, they fail to see the easier two-stage method of obtaining 20 quarts.

As we saw when considering "sameness and difference", similarities may be more or less remote and with human subjects it may sometimes be desirable to hasten and extend generalization across widely separated situations by providing verbal links. There is some evidence that what is called "teaching for transfer" works well (Hovland, 1951), by calling attention to other situations in which learning may be applied. On the other hand, problem-solving work has tended to stress the value of allowing the learner to discover general solutions for himself.

However, giving a solution and allowing it to be inferred both gave similar scores in experiments on oddity problems by Craig (1956), and on cryptographic code problems (Haslerud and Meyers, 1958). Kittell (1957) favours "intermediate direction", in which the work of formulating the relevant principle is begun by the trainer and continued by the student. It is clear in any case that a great deal depends upon the ability of the individual learner and upon the level at which the principle is couched.

The best level of generality of any verbal formula will depend upon what the object of the training is. For a specific task, it was shown in the earlier chapter on "words and actions" that any instruction should be simple and directly applicable, and the same conclusion probably applies here. In other cases it may be the object to provide training of a wide, general nature. The traditional doctrine of "formal discipline" held that the learning of subjects like Latin and geometry generally improved the mind. It must be admitted that this hypothesis is not really tested by experiments which show little transfer from the formal subjects to special areas of knowledge or special abilities (Thorndike, 1924), since only a complete survey of the life of a formally disciplined individual would be adequate; the analysis of transfer by Meredith (1941) makes clear the variety of methodological and semantic difficulties which beset this kind of experiment.

Most training schemes have humbler aims, and here it is clear that any wholesale recourse to teaching by abstract principles is unnecessary. There is little point in teaching formal electronic theory to a radio mechanic; there are more efficient ways of preparing him for the job, as the series of texts by Van Valkenburgh, Nooger and

Neville (1959) may show. Successful training depends heavily upon deciding exactly what is to be taught, and taking appropriate direct steps to teach it. Systematic methods of exploiting this approach are described in the following chapter.

SUMMARY

Carrying over learning from one task to another is known as transfer of training. If the old learning helps on the new task transfer is *positive* and if it hinders transfer is *negative*. Learning a new task may also affect previous learning through what is known as retroaction. Both transfer and retroaction depend upon the degree of similarity between tasks. Effective similarity is partly learned, and varies from individual to individual and from one time to another.

Effects of similarity. Dividing continuous tasks into separate stimuli and responses is somewhat artificial, but gives us a rule of thumb for predicting transfer. If two tasks require the same responses transfer and retroaction will be highly positive when the same stimuli are presented, and less positive as the stimuli are made less similar. More learning will give more transfer. Changing the required responses while leaving the stimuli essentially the same will tend to give negative transfer.

Negative transfer. Mistakes will tend to occur when the subject is not sure which response is appropriate to a given stimulus. This kind of confusion is often observed when (1) responses are similar but differ in a way which affects the scoring or the practical results of the task, and (2) when the same set of responses is rearranged with respect to the stimuli. Negative transfer is accompanied by, or may develop into, positive transfer. Variety of practice materials soon overcomes negative transfer and produces flexible performance.

Task difficulty. Transfer may be *unequal* between two tasks of different difficulty. What happens in detail depends upon what constitutes the "difficulty". As a broad generalization it is suggested that any particular outcome depends upon two opposing tendencies (1) towards better transfer from difficult tasks which give wider experience, and (2) towards better transfer from easier tasks which produce more accurate learning.

Principles. It is recognized that the similarities which determine human transfer may be less specific than direct physical resemblances between stimuli and responses. Verbalization of broad similarities by the subject may extend transfer, but how far the trainer should impose verbal formulations is in doubt. The generality of any verbal teaching should be related to the purposes of training.

8. PROGRAMMED LEARNING

IN AN ideal training situation, instruction would be systematically designed. Each learner would be given new material at a rate which suited him, and of a kind which he could patently master at his current stage of learning. The few mistakes which occurred would be quickly corrected, and his progress would be evident to himself and to the trainer. All the factors which determine the outcome of training would be easy to discern, control and modify, and the training scheme would be constantly upgraded by revision.

These are in fact the aims of automatic teaching, or "programmed instruction". Often, the requisite degree of control over the presentation and handling of the teaching material has seemed to necessitate the use of mechanical devices, even for verbal learning, and it is with these instructional engines that the account of programmed learning begins.

TEACHING MACHINES

Pressey (1927) described the possibilities for teaching of the machine illustrated in Fig. 34 (left, second row). Here, a question appears in the window of the apparatus together with four possible answers. For instance, "To help the poor debtors of England, James Oglethorpe founded the colony of

(1) Connecticut,
(2) Delaware,
(3) Maryland,
(4) Georgia."

The answers are lettered to correspond with the response keys. When the subject presses the correct key, the drum holding the questions revolves and a new question appears; should he press the wrong key, the drum does not move, and the same question remains until the right key is pressed. The apparatus could be adjusted to present a series of questions as many times as needed. It had originally been intended to use this kind of machine for *testing*, but it soon became evident that students could *learn* from operating it, since they could not proceed without discovering the right answer to each question.

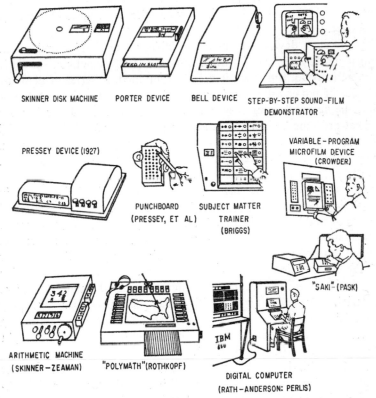

SKINNER DISK MACHINE   PORTER DEVICE   BELL DEVICE   STEP-BY-STEP SOUND-FILM DEMONSTRATOR

PRESSEY DEVICE (1927)

PUNCHBOARD (PRESSEY, ET AL)   SUBJECT MATTER TRAINER (BRIGGS)

VARIABLE-PROGRAM MICROFILM DEVICE (CROWDER)

"SAKI" (PASK)

ARITHMETIC MACHINE (SKINNER–ZEAMAN)   "POLYMATH" (ROTHKOPF)

DIGITAL COMPUTER (RATH–ANDERSON: PERLIS)

FIG. 34. Various forms of teaching machine. From Lumsdaine (1959).

Pressey's machines were largely neglected, and current interest springs from Skinner's (1954) article in which the accumulated research of the learning laboratory is applied to educational techniques. Skinner's early machine (Fig. 34; left, top row) presents information and questions, or rather forms of words which prompt an answer, which are mounted on a circular disc. The subject matter may vary from nuclear physics to civil defence, or from genetics to rhetoric. As each question appears the student writes an answer on a paper tape next to the question window and raises a lever. His answer then moves up under a transparent cover, which prevents alterations, to appear alongside the correct answer. If his own answer is correct he moves the lever to the right, which marks his answer record and brings into view the next question in the sequence.

Many such devices are now available, some simpler and others considerably more complicated. Porter's (1958) machine, shown in Fig. 34 (second, top row), is greatly simplified. A series of items on a sheet of paper are moved up by a lever one at a time, the same sheet being used as an answer blank by the student. There is some "cheat-proofing", since the student's responses are again protected by a transparent cover when the answer appears, but no provision for "drop-out" of correctly answered questions when the cycle of questions is presented for a second time.

Far more elaborate arrangements are provided by filmstrip projection devices of the kind described by Crowder (1960) and shown at middle right in Fig. 34. Frames giving short sequences of information are presented singly; following scrutiny of the frame, the subject presses a response button which determines the character of the information next to be presented. The machine contains sequences affording a number of different routes through the subject material. Even greater flexibility may be introduced by using electronic computers as teaching machines; by suitable programming it can be arranged that a large number of students may all be taught at the same time (Coulson, 1962).

For some kinds of subject matter it is desirable to gather together a number of different apparatus facilities. In the "language laboratories", for instance, machines bearing written programmes of instruction in vocabulary and grammar usually take second place to tape recording devices. Playing over oral lessons allows the student to hear authentic pronunciation and idiom; if self-recording is available also, he can hear his own attempts and compare them with those of the expert.

MOTOR LEARNING

Many training devices which provide for the learning of motor skills are "teaching machines" in a loose sense. The mediaeval "quintain" is one. This was an arrangement presenting a shield as target to an armed knight. If he hit the centre the shield fell over, but if struck askew it delivered a retributive blow of the flail as the knight rode past. Other examples of synthetic training are provided by devices like the gunnery simulator discussed earlier (Goldstein and Rittenhouse, 1954) or by various aircraft ground trainers. In most cases no elaborate pedagogical principles have informed the design of the equipment.

In the manual task trainers of Pask (1958) the mechanisms used are "adaptive"; the performance demanded of the trainee varies in quite a detailed way as learning proceeds. To teach keyboard operations such as typewriting or punched card preparation, use is made of visual guidance in the form of an indicator light showing which key should be depressed for each item of an exercise (Fig. 34; lower right). The machine records and assesses the efficiency of performance and, as the trainee becomes more proficient, varies the pace of work. The more successful the performance, the faster the rate demanded; if the learner becomes inefficient the pace may be slowed.

Further, the machine will discriminate between difficult and easy keys, so that difficult symbols remain indicated for a longer time than easy ones. Again, the adaptability of the machine allows the criterion of ease or difficulty to be adjusted for the individual operator. The machine also shows flexibility with respect to the presence or absence of guidance, so that the visual indication may be withdrawn completely as individual keys are learned. This is one form of "vanishing", or "fading", which can also be employed in teaching the tracing of maps or circuit diagrams (Holland, 1960). These principles appear desirable and, although there is no formal evidence in their support, are in accord with the aims outlined earlier in this chapter.

No other examples of automatic methods in motor learning are available and, since the major effort in programmed instruction has been directed towards verbal learning, it is to verbal programmes that the discussion returns.

LINEAR PROGRAMMES

Teaching machines are devices for presenting programmes, and the value of these machines depends largely upon the programming principles which they embody. Programmes, in this context, are the sequences of items which convey the required information to the learner. For reasons of convenience and economy they are often published separately in the form of "scrambled textbooks", which may be studied without machine presentation. In the book form of programme the correct answers are usually separated spatially from the questions to which they correspond.

There may be some loss in efficiency when the machines are omitted, as has been shown for one kind of programme in teaching trigonometry to naval electricians (Wallis and Wicks, 1963), although the difference is relatively small. The machines themselves add novelty, but it is not yet clear how transitory is the resultant incentive value. The error scores in the naval study suggest that the lack of cheat-proofing, permitting trainees to look at the answer before formulating a response, contributed to the inferior showing of the scrambled text. Unfortunately, the appropriate machines are often costly and bulky, and require programme material in an unstandardized variety of formats.

Instructional programmes differ from spoken lectures, and from conventional textbooks, in several important ways. The subject material is broken into sequences of short items, each presenting one new fact or idea. Conceptual information is built up by showing a new idea in a number of different ways through several items or frames. Each item both prompts and requires an answer from the student. The answers are immediately checked, so that knowledge of being right "reinforces" the acquired learning. Since the material develops logically and the questions prompt or "cue" the correct answer, the student nearly always is right. Thus, the theory runs, the learner is actively attentive throughout the course. His activity is regularly rewarded and he is gradually led from stage to stage in a way which leads to few misconceptions or failures.

A sample of programmed material on the subject of heaving the lead is shown in Table 4. This kind of programme is a *linear* one, since all students are expected to progress through the items in the same, fixed order. The example programme has not been tried out in practice and revised, as all programmes intended for use should be, and probably contains infelicities of design. Although it may be

TABLE 4. Extract from an imaginary linear programme

Sentence to be Completed	Correct Answer
STEP 21 Six marks appear in the first ten fathoms. Some depths are unmarked, but six are indicated by	marks
STEP 22 The first three depths are all marked. There are marks at 1 fathom, 2 fathoms and	3 fathoms
STEP 23 The marks at 1, 2 and 3 fathoms are leathers. At 1 fathom there is 1 leather tag. There are 2 leather tags at 2 fathoms, and .... leather tags at 3 fathoms.	3 (three)
STEP 24 The depth of 4 fathoms is unmarked. There are marks at 1, 2 and 3 fathoms, but .... mark at 4 fathoms.	no
STEP 25 An unmarked depth is known as a *deep*. For instance, 4 fathoms is unmarked and is thus a	deep
STEP 26 The mark at 5 fathoms is a white calico tag. When a white tag appears at the waterline, the sounding is shown as .... by the mark.	five (5)
STEP 27 The deeps are estimated from the next highest mark. If the mark 5 is out of the water, the water will be .... down the leadline, and the actual depth will be .... than 5 fathoms.	lower less
STEP 28 If the white mark 5 appears about a fathom above the waterline, the water is only 4 fathoms	deep

desirable to allow the student to make a few errors, in order to heighten the value of correct responses by contrast, good design depends upon keeping the error rate low. Assuming that the order of presentation of the subject matter is logical, a low error rate will depend principally upon breaking the material into steps of the right size, and upon using efficient prompting techniques.

PROGRAMME CHARACTERISTICS

Step size is not easy to describe in quantitative terms, although Green (1962) has suggested a measure of "program density" which shows the number of different responses required by the programme as a proportion of the total number of responses used. An easy technique for varying step size is to drop out some of the units or frames, making the gap between these items larger. Coulson and Silberman (1959) compared small-step programmes in experimental psychology with large-step equivalents having about half the number of frames. A written test showed that small steps resulted in better learning, at the expense of longer training time.

Longer total times were needed for the small steps in the study by Evans, Glaser and Homme (1959), who investigated sequences consisting of 30, 40, 51 or 68 steps. Although learning tended to improve as the number of steps increased, the 68-step programme was no better than the one with 51 steps. One might expect little improvement beyond a certain number of steps and, in fact, Smith and Moore (1962) found no differences in a spelling programme between a range of step sizes which all used several frames to each spelled word.

As the example in Table 4 implies, the prompting of correct responses is typically so extreme as to "give the answer away". Correct responses are confirmed after they have been made, but this subsequent confirmation plays less important a part in a programme than the preceding prompting. The issue of confirmation versus prompting is analogous to the issue of knowledge of results versus guidance. The potential value of verbal guidance was considered earlier (Chapter 5), and we may expect the technique of prompting to be reasonably effective. An explicit comparison of pure confirmation versus pure prompting may be made by giving the correct answer either before or after the subject has responded to each of a series of stimuli. Under these conditions Cook (1963) reports that giving the answer beforehand is at least as good as knowledge of results in teaching word-pairing, and better on a punchboard task (Fig. 35). Further research on the best amount of cueing or prompting is in progress in several laboratories.

Prompting can take many forms in a teaching programme. Homme and Glaser (1959) suggest that the most common and most important method may be formalized as the "ruleg" system, in which examples are prompted by preceding rules. "Ruleg" stands for "rule" and "e.g." or example. Thus, in the sample programme (Table 4) we give the rule, "An unmarked depth is known as a *deep*"; this cues the response to, "For instance, 4 fathoms is

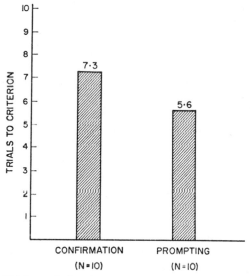

Fig. 35. Trials needed to learn a punchboard task by confirmation or prompting methods. From Cook (1963).

unmarked and is thus a ...." However, many other forms of prompt appear useful.

The serial properties of numbers may be used: "There are marks at 1 fathom, 2 fathoms and ...." Word habits are useful, as in: ". . . the water is only 4 fathoms ...." Some prompts are echoic, using the repetition of a word or words: "The mark at 5 fathoms . . . is shown as .... by the mark." Yet another technique is the use of contrasts: "Some depths are *unmarked*, but six are indicated by ...." Other kinds of prompt involve the use of analogies, comparison between frames or reference to the preceding frame. What matters is whether they work, and this can always be discovered by testing the programme.

BRANCHING PROGRAMMES

In the linear, or Skinner-type, programmes the object of the programme designer is to avert errors. An alternative course of action is to cater for a modicum of errors, using the information about the learner which a particular error reveals in order to lead him through appropriate extra material. Different kinds of error will require different remedial treatment, so that different learners will take different routes through the programme material. Programmes which offer alternative routes are *branching*, or Crowder-type, programmes. They were first designed for use in the electronic filmstrip teaching machines described earlier, but have also been successful as scrambled textbooks on subjects like the arithmetic of computers (Crowder, 1962).

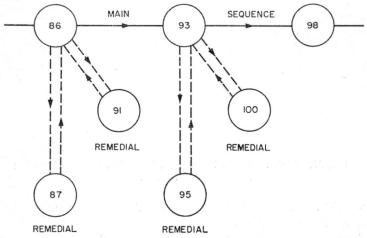

FIG. 36. Simple branching. The numbers used correspond with the example pages in Table 5.

A scrambled textbook on programming by Cram (1961) uses both techniques; linear sections of the book describe linear methods, and branching sections describe branching methods. Simple branching principles are illustrated schematically in Fig. 36 and an example of scrambled textbook design, purporting to deal with traditional formal logic, is given in Table 5. The sequence of moves is as follows: Having responded correctly to a previous question, the student arrives at page 86 of the example. He digests the new material, and selects one of the alternative answers to the question at the foot of the page. If his answer is correct, he turns to page 93 and continues through the programme. If he chooses a wrong answer, he turns to page 87 or page 91, where he finds out that he was wrong and what it was that was wrong. This remedial material may be much more elaborate than in the example shown. He then returns to our arbitrary starting point at page 86 and chooses another answer. If he is right, he proceeds to page 93 and the cycle begins again. The various routes are thus an integral part of the programme; Crowder refers to this kind of design as "intrinsic programming'"

Of course, it is possible to devise much more complicated forms of branching. As Crowder (1960) shows, we may arrange that a particularly bad error will "wash back" the student to an earlier

TABLE 5. Extract from an imaginary branching text

                                                           Page 86
Your Answer: A universal negative proposition   (from page 82)

Good. The next kind of immediate inference is *obversion*. We have learned to consider all propositions as consisting of a subject term (S) and a predicate (P). Now we must understand the use of *not*-P. If P stands for "solids", then not-P stands for everything else in the universe. It would be wrong to interpret not-P as "liquids" or "gases" or any other particular class of entities. Although it seems rather clumsy, the term not-P is best read as *other-than*-P.

Now, if "all S is P" means "all pondenomes are grocid", what is the meaning of "all S is not-P"?
Answer

No pondenomes are grocid	Page 87
Everything other than pondenomes is grocid	Page 91
All pondenomes are other than grocid	Page 93

                                                           Page 87
Your Answer: No pondenomes are grocid   (from page 86)

You are running ahead too far. What you have given is the *contrary* relation, which you will be shown later. Remember, in obversion we do not want to negate the whole proposition. We merely want to consider those things which are excluded from P. Turn back to page 86, read the material there carefully and choose another answer.

TABLE 5. *Continued*

Page 91
Your Answer: Everything other than pondenomes   (from page 86)
is grocid

You have the right idea, but you have started at the wrong end
of the sentence. What you have done is to obvert the *subject* term
of the proposition instead of its *predicate*. You have given as your
answer "not-*S* is *P*". What we want is "all *S* is not-*P*". Return to
page 86 and try again.

Page 93
Your Answer: All pondenomes are other than grocid   (from page 86)

That is correct. Now that we know how to handle the term *not*-P,
we can go on to see which obverse inferences are valid. Let us try
again with "all *S* is *P*". This time, let us make it equal to: "all
Martians are imaginary beings". Well, if all Martians are imaginary
beings, clearly it must be true that *no* Martians are *other than*
imaginary beings. Using *not*-P is a way of excluding things from the
class named in the predicate. Because all Martians are included in
the class of imaginary beings, naturally none of them is excluded.
So that the obverse of "all *S* is *P*" is "no *S* is not-*P*". Let us try an
example. If it is true that "all flatworms are cannibals", what is the
obverse?
Answer
  Not all cannibals are flatworms   Page 95
  No flatworms are other than cannibals   Page 98
  What *are* flatworms?   Page 100

---

part of the programme; or we may also "wash forward" a particularly bright student, so that the whole procedure resembles the game
of snakes and ladders. On the whole, the number and kind of
subsequences which are inserted will depend upon the "audience"
for which the programme is intended. Many subsequences may be
appropriate for a mixed group of learners, while groups of uniform
background and calibre will be well served by a relatively straightforward programme.

Table 5 shows other features which, in practice, are typical of
branching programmes. Not necessarily, but often, the step size is
larger than we find in linear programmes. The frames tend to be
longer, and often include the juxtaposition of several ideas or
principles. Even more important is the use of "prefabricated"
answers. In order to prepare in advance alternative, remedial

material which will be appropriate for certain kinds of error, we must somehow limit the number of branches provided. We cannot budget for an indefinite number of error pathways, and the easiest solution is to lay down a schedule of permissible errors. In this way, the branching programme becomes a kind of multiple-choice test. The student working through a *linear* programme constructs his own responses.

One way of reconciling the principle of branching with the constructed response technique has been discovered (Kay, Annett and Sime, 1963) and used in the Sheffield teaching machine. The student writes his own response on a card and inserts it into the machine to bring about the display of the correct answer. He decides whether his answer is correct or not, and then presses one of the buttons which route him to the next part of the programme. If his answer was wrong, he presses a button marked "?" which presents a remedial subsequence. This device appears to embody a very reasonable theoretical combination of characteristics. However, most branching programmes do use the multiple-choice response technique.

COMPARISON OF METHODS

Branching different learners through appropriate sequences of material has the appearance of being a flexible and enlightened procedure. However, enthusiasts for the linear techniques argue that what we are trying to do is teach people to make responses for themselves, not to read the responses which are printed for them. It therefore seems more appropriate that they should practise making their own responses during training; the multiple-choice technique offers a mere recognition task, which seems less conducive to learning. In fact, recognizing something is always easier than trying to recall it, and it may be for this reason that "branched" students can apparently handle a larger step size. If less is expected of the branched student, while he is exposed to more material between responses, it seems plausible that his learning should be "thinner".

What is more, it is argued, the labour spent in anticipating and providing for errors in branching programmes might be better devoted to writing these errors out of the programme. In a linear programme this is done by inserting extra steps wherever preliminary testing shows that errors accumulate. Again, if the alternative routes of the branching programme are to be useful, the erroneous answers which lead to them must be plausible. We do not want the learner to practise making errors, but if the alternatives laid out beside the correct answer are plausible, the programme is actually prompting errors.

These arguments seem cogent enough, although the experimental facts seem less dramatic. One difficulty is that it is not clear that the

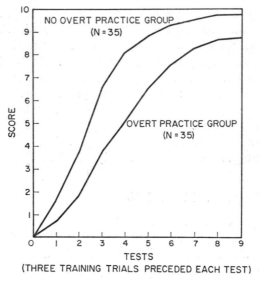

FIG. 37. Learning with and without responding. From Cook (1963).

student cannot learn without responding overtly; he may respond "in his head". We have already seen that implicit responses play an effective part in mental practice. Cook (1963) has discussed the contribution made by overt responses in verbal learning, in order to clarify the principles of programming. Figure 37 shows the difference between two groups learning pairs of words, one group being required to make overt responses, the other not. In this study, the learners who did *not* respond were slightly better.

However, it is only if the student responds openly that we can be sure he is attending actively. In a multiple-choice programme, he *may* construct his own implicit response before selecting one of the alternatives, but it is technically possible for him to work through the programme by a series of completely random choices. The results of teaching by branching methods may sometimes be rather less efficient, depending upon how the student has used the programme. In a study by Fry (1960) the teaching of Spanish was attempted by both constructed-response and multiple-choice methods. On an immediate test, and on a test of recall two days later, the constructed-response method gave better results. If both groups were allowed to complete the programme, the constructed-response group took nearly twice as long as the multiple-choice group but, given the same amount of time, constructed-response still appeared better.

In Coulson and Silberman's (1959) experiment on the teaching of experimental psychology, the multiple-choice problem and the branching problem were both investigated. Branching, by a "wash-forward" method in which successful subjects omitted a number of items, took less time on the average than linear programmes and gave roughly the same amount of learning. Multiple-choice also took less time for almost the same results as were obtained by constructed-response. However, the best single result in the learning scores was obtained with the combination of constructed-response and a linear programme.

EVALUATION

Programmed methods in general compare very favourably with classroom teaching. It is difficult to decide exactly how much advantage is gained, since one is usually comparing a particular programme with a particular teacher, and both of these may be good or bad. A further complication is that devising a programme enforces great clarity upon the author. Thus, programming improves the programmer, and if he is also the teacher the comparison becomes artificial.

Enough studies have been performed to leave no doubt that both kinds of programme work well, often with considerable saving of time spent in learning and, of course, in teaching. With branching programmes, examples of the comparison between automatic and classroom methods are provided by the naval (Wallis and Wicks, 1963), air force (Knight, 1963) and civil airline studies (Cavanagh, Thornton and Morgan, 1963). Better learning with linear programmes than with traditional methods is shown by Ripple (1963),

Engstrom and Whittaker (1963) and others. In fact, Kay, Annett and Sime (1963) summarize as many as forty-two evaluation studies, most of which show machine teaching to advantage.

The great advantage of programmed learning lies in its objectivity. The whole process of learning is laid open to inspection at any point so that, as is said of philosophy, the remedy for bad programmes is better programmes. Frames may be added or taken away, or choices inserted; bad prompts may be made unambiguous, or the prompting may be reduced so that the learner does more of the work. The whole procedure lends itself to detailed revision and improvement in a way that is not possible with traditional methods. If one gives a bad talk, the details of what was said and what went wrong are usually not on record. The programmer gets knowledge of results of a kind and quantity which is not available to the classroom teacher or lecturer.

The human teacher is also at a disadvantage inasmuch as his output is directed at a group of learners whose capacities for learning vary. Students of teaching programmes can always progress to new material at a rate which suits their individual readiness. Admittedly the method is impersonal and not immediately acceptable to everyone, although one imagines that a growing familiarity with teaching machines will gradually disperse a great many apprehensions and misapprehensions. Teaching machines are not intended to replace the human teacher, but to do certain teaching jobs carefully, quickly and well. Used sensibly, there is little doubt that teaching machines can contribute a great deal. The principles upon which they are based are equally important, and may be embodied in many different kinds of training.

SUMMARY

Teaching machines are devices for presenting programmes of pre-arranged items of information. They elicit responses from the student and provide automatic knowledge of results. Many degrees of elaboration are possible in their design.

Programmes. Whether presented by machines or in the form of *programmed textbooks*, instructional programmes are intended to permit individual learners to make responses at their own rates. A high proportion of the student's responses are right, because the forms of words which constitute the programme items or steps are designed to *prompt* the correct answers. The steps which make up the programme are arranged in an orderly sequence, and are preferably of a size and kind determined by preliminary trials to lead the learner efficiently from the known to the unknown. Up to a point the smaller the size of step the better.

Branching. If the programme consists of a single sequence of steps it is classified as *linear*; if making an error routes the learner through extra sequences of material the programme is *branching*. With branching methods students are usually given multiple-choice alternatives and larger step size. Linear programmes require the student to construct his own responses; they typically consist of smaller steps, and tend to encourage a lower error rate. Linear programmes therefore seem theoretically preferable, although in practice the differences are not great.

Effectiveness. Teaching machines and learning programmes do teach, usually with some saving in time and effort, by a combination of guidance, practice and knowledge of results. Although there are few examples of programming for motor skills the usefulness of programmed methods is not restricted to verbal learning, since these methods have been developed from the basic principles of training.

9. RECOMMENDATIONS

WHAT we have done so far is to consider the available research evidence bearing upon the problems of training. This is a reasonable procedure since it does give a solid basis for examining further the detailed problems of training particular skills, but it has two disadvantages. One of them is that things have been left out. By and large a topic has not been discussed if it has not received experimental treatment.

Maxims like "keep your eye on the ball" are probably valuable in many games, but do not seem to have attracted any research. "Keep your eye on the nail" seems to express a parallel truth for hammering. Very likely these statements should draw our attention to the way in which the kinaesthetic control of movement is interlinked with the visual frame of reference, but the necessary work has not been carried out. Thus, while what has been said in earlier chapters is the experimental truth it is certainly not the whole truth.

The other disadvantage is the lack of simple, definite recommendations to the trainer. This deficit is due both to the incompleteness of existing research and to the fact that learning and training are complicated matters. There are no simple "golden rules". Such rules as do emerge tend to be abstract and provisional, but yet can give some guidance towards better training.

GENERAL

The job of the trainer is to *observe* and *analyse*, and to arrange to supply the right amount of the right kind of *information* to the learner at the right time. He must know a great deal about the task being trained, but the kind of knowledge needed is what comes from careful, objective analyses of the job and of the necessary skill rather than from the experience of becoming personally proficient. His task is to find out what factors affect the learning of the skill with which he is concerned, to watch the effects of varying them and to try to arrange the best combination.

Other training considerations flow from an accurate analysis of the job. The trainer must be completely clear as to what he is trying to teach and the learner must be completely clear as to what he is set to learn. If the task is precise and easily specified so much the better, but it is also possible to be clear about jobs which involve several functions or a flexibility of performance, and thus to train the learner to meet a variety of situations. Fortunately, clarity of purpose is one of the by-products of evaluation, of seeing how training measures work out. In any practical situation the trainer will have to try the effects of applying principles which seem appropriate to his problems. Measuring the effects of any changes will require the setting up of *criteria* of success, such as the ability to wind two centre-tapped mains transformers per day to acceptable electrical standards, and deciding upon such criteria inevitably helps the trainer to shape his programme.

Evaluating the training programme as a whole, and experimenting with detailed changes, are part of the trainer's responsibility. Although it has been admitted that sophisticated, formal experiments are out of place in a practical training scheme, there is no reason why adjustments should not be made in a systematic way. One of the basic rules for discovering the effects of different factors is to *vary one thing at a time*. For a number of reasons this may not always be possible, but it is worth approximating to this ideal when making changes. If a training film is introduced at the same time that training is restricted to mornings only and the equipment is changed, no one can disentangle the various effects.

Once it is clear what the object of training is, a number of decisions must be made concerning the most plausible methods for trial. It must be decided how much verbal knowledge is required as a background to carrying out the job and how it is to be taught, whether special equipment is needed and what form it should take. These problems merge into all the more detailed considerations which were discussed earlier. Instructions, hints, guidance of various kinds, perceptual cues from the task, visual aids, knowledge of results and scores may all be viewed as forms of information which impinge upon the learner, so that our objective may be stated as one of regulating his supply of information. Underloading the learner is wasteful, but overloading him is all too easy an error to commit. Ideally he should be given as much as he can absorb or process at any stage, bearing in mind that his capacity for dealing with information will change as learning proceeds.

SPECIFIC

How far one should provide a background of verbal knowledge is never an easy decision to make. Where the task requires a theoretical background, as where some knowledge of the properties of inductance and resistance is needed for "bespoke" transformer-winding, it is worth considering presenting this knowledge by *programmed methods*. Care should be taken explicitly to relate theoretical issues to practical operations. It is also worth taking pains to remove part of this information load from the operator by arranging a permanent *display* of necessary data; probably visual aids are at their best used in this way rather than for training purposes.

Other tasks requiring less knowledge, like the job of making soundings with a leadline which was used as an earlier illustration, may or may not need verbal preparation. In such cases it will often be true that verbal practice is less appropriate than it appears and that *"activity" methods* provide a good solution. Most verbal methods are powerful, but for that very reason may be over-employed. In any case many trainees will be less verbally inclined than the trainer.

The study of "verbal pre-training" has been largely a laboratory concern, although there is no doubt that *knowing the names* of things is a fundamental requirement for many learners. In the instructional film training on sashcord assembly mentioned earlier, a common complaint was that there was insufficient time to assimilate the names of parts. Another difficulty of film presentation is that the whole task is presented symbolically before the learner has a chance to practise, thus forming a long sequence of instructions. Detailed instructions may be harmful in continuous tasks, and in most tasks are probably best broken into snatches of *verbal guidance* inserted as the task proceeds—"first, take the carvel boss in your right hand . . . now, push once with your foot to bring the gasset spline into position . . . and press home the locking spigot."

If practice is preceded by a demonstration it is important that the instructor does not restrict himself to showing only the movement, but draws attention to the *perceptual cues* he is using. For example, it may not be obvious that he is adjusting for contrast rather than for brightness. In many skills, where the timing of responses is crucial, these will often be preceded by *advance cues*. Pointing these out saves time in preparing the response and helps the co-ordination of performance. Care must be taken that the analysis of the operation is complete. The "feel" of an operation is often important, as in cutting a thread on a bolt with a die, and it is therefore necessary to draw attention to *kinaesthetic* and tactile cues.

Sometimes the necessary cues may be amplified or *magnified*, or extra indications added to the equipment. It can be arranged that pressing too hard on a drill sounds a horn, or that tilting a javelin interrupts a light beam which rings a bell, but such devices must be designed and presented in such a way as to draw attention to the relevant *intrinsic cues*. Otherwise they may be used as concurrent feedback and relied upon to the detriment of permanent learning. Adding extra cues in the form of *visual guidance* has much to commend it, although far more research is needed to establish the boundaries of this technique.

If physical guidance methods are used care must be taken to ensure that the actions made during training are compatible with those required on the task, and that information concerning *alternative* responses is not excluded. Very often a little preliminary unguided experience may be advisable. Since it is easy to misguide by forced-response methods, and since these methods may need more instrumentation, techniques of *restriction* will often be chosen as a means of reducing early errors. One or two laboratory tasks have been learned in their entirety by guidance training, but it is more usual to complete learning by the successive correction of residual errors.

Trial-and-error learning depends upon successive correction, usually by the *knowledge of results* which is inherent in the task. The trainer can help to draw attention to the relation between particular kinds of action and the appropriate feedback, and help in recognizing feedback cues and the stimulus conditions which lead up to certain outcomes. The kinds of knowledge of results which are added artificially seem to work best when they are indirect. Letting the learner know where he stands by assessing his *progress*, discussing and analysing his faults and waiting until his actions are completed before correcting them are all valuable methods. Analysing faults can often be helped by the use of recording instruments.

Of course, some situations offer virtually no intrinsic knowledge of results, not because there is no feedback but because there are no *standards* against which to assess it. In learning to send Morse code we may read the stimulus "*P*" and respond by sending "dash, dot, dot, dash". Intrinsic feedback will help us to regulate the length and spacing of the dots and dashes, but will not inform us that what should have been sent was "dot, dash, dash, dot", since this is arbitrary. Here again the trainer must arrange to supply the information, preferably item-by-item. He must also supply the standards for evaluating the learner's progress on a long-term basis throughout practice.

The way in which practice periods are distributed does not seem a serious practical issue since the differences between massed and spaced practice are likely to be small within a reasonable range of work distributions, although it is clearly sensible to arrange a break when the learner shows signs of *fatigue*. Long rest pauses are unlikely to do harm by allowing forgetting to occur, but the temptation is to fill them with some other activity. Under some circumstances this may cause *interference* with the main task, just as may happen with incompatible previous training. Interference from closely similar activities will disappear with further learning, but may cause trouble if errors are important. Spacing practice periods allows time for subjects to engage in *mental practice*, which should be explicitly encouraged.

Practising the *parts* of a task separately is useful unless the task is changed by the process of subdivision. In fact most tasks worth learning need to be subdivided, in accordance with the principle of optimizing the load placed upon the learner. Much car-driving instruction, for example, is carried out by having the learner practise the steering component separately from the gear-changing activities. Where tasks are only awkwardly divisible into parts, as in high-diving, it seems reasonable to attain them by *gradual progression*.   Raising the diving platform by inches as learning proceeds is analogous to building mathematical knowledge by careful programming.

At every stage of programmed learning the trainee is asked to do only what is within his grasp. He is *prompted* throughout and *corrected* where necessary, but has chosen the response himself on the basis of the information available to him. The right amount of information is available, because the programmer knows what he is trying to achieve and has experimented with ways of achieving it. In the same way we may hope to create efficiently programmed training.

FURTHER READING

PSYCHOLOGICAL texts on learning theory tend to examine the general theory of behaviour rather than problems of learning and will, in any case, be known to the technical reader. The present selection consists of books dealing explicitly with training and skill.

A practical account of methods of industrial training is given by:

SEYMOUR, W. D. *Industrial Training for Manual Operations.* Pitman, London (1954).

A general introduction to experimental psychology, in which perceptual and motor skills and abilities are stressed, is:

GAGNÉ, R. M. and FLEISHMAN, E. A. *Psychology and Human Performance.* Holt, New York (1959).

A book on learning and skill whose interest extends far beyond its ostensible concern with physical education is:

KNAPP, B. *Skill in Sport.* Routledge, London (1963).

A more difficult book, in which human skills are searchingly analysed, is:

WELFORD, A. T. *Ageing and Human Skill.* Oxford U.P., London (1958).

The series of booklets issued by the Department of Scientific and Industrial Research present the results of recent research simply and clearly:

Problems of Progress in Industry. H.M.S.O., London.

REFERENCES
and Author Index

(*The figures in brackets immediately following each reference show the number of the page in this book in which the reference is used.*)

ADAMS, J. A. (1954) Psychomotor response acquisition and transfer as a function of control–indicator relationships, *J. exp. Psychol.* **48**, 10–18. (107, 111)

ADAMS, J. A. (1955) A source of decrement in psychomotor skill, *J. exp. Psychol.* **49**, 390–394. (60)

ADAMSON, G. T. (1959) Circuit training, *Ergonomics*, **2**, 183–186. (10)

ALEXANDER, L. T., KEPNER, C. H. and TREGOE, B. B. (1962) The effectiveness of knowledge of results in a military system-training program, *J. appl, Psychol.* **46**, 02–211. (33)

ALONZO, A. S. (1926) The influence of manual guidance upon maze learning, *J. comp. Psychol.* **6**, 143–158. (40)

AMMONS, R. B., AMMONS, C. H. and MORGAN, R. L. (1956) Transfer of skill and decremental factors along the speed dimension in rotary pursuit, *Percept. mot. Skills*, **6**, 43. (113)

ANNETT, J. (1959) Learning a pressure under conditions of immediate and delayed knowledge of results, *Quart. J. exp. Psychol.* **11**, 3–15. (26, 30, 39)

ANNETT, J. and KAY, H. (1957) Knowledge of results and skilled performance, *Occup. Psychol.* **31**, 69–79. (17)

ANTHONY, W. S., HOLDING, D. H., SLUCKIN, W. and LION, J. S. (1962) Size–weight interaction in judgments of compound stimuli, *Quart. J. exp. Psychol.* **14**, 77–88. (77)

ARCHER, E. J. (1954) Postrest performance in motor learning as a function of prerest degree of distribution of practice, *J. exp. Psychol.* **47**, 47–51. (96)

ARCHER, E. J. and BOURNE, L. E. (1956) Inverted-alphabet printing as a function of intertrial rest and sex, *J. exp. Psychol.* **52**, 322–328. (97)

ARNOULT, M. D. (1957) Stimulus predifferentiation: some generalizations and hypotheses, *Psychol. Bull.* **54**, 339–350. (76)

ARPS, G. F. (1917) A preliminary report on work with knowledge versus work without knowledge of results, *Psychol. Rev.* **24**, 449–455. (20)

BAKER, K. E. and WYLIE, R. C. (1950) Transfer of verbal training to a motor task, *J. exp. Psychol.* **40**, 632–638. (77)

BAKER, K. E., WYLIE, R. C. and GAGNÉ, R. M. (1950) Transfer of training to a motor skill as a function of variation in the rate of response, *J. exp. Psychol.* **40**, 721–732. (113)

143

BAKER, R. A. and OSGOOD, S. W. (1954) Discrimination training along a pitch continuum, *J. exp. Psychol.* **48**, 241–246. (113)

BARTON, J. W. (1921) Small vs. larger units in learning the maze, *J. exp. Psychol.* **4**, 418–429. (90, 91)

BATESON, G. and MEAD, M. (1942) *Balinese Culture: A Photographic Analysis.* N.Y. Acad. Sci., New York. (38)

BATTIG, W. F. (1954) The effect of kinesthetic, verbal and visual cues on the acquisition of a lever-positioning skill, *J. exp. Psychol.* **47**, 371–380. (79)

BELBIN, E. (1956). The effects of propaganda on recall, recognition and behaviour. II. The conditions which determine the response to propaganda, *Brit. J. Psychol.* **47**, 259–270. (71)

BELBIN, E. (1958) Methods of training older workers, *Ergonomics*, **1**, 207–221. (59, 71)

BELBIN, E., BELBIN, R. M. and HILL, F. (1957) A comparison between the results of three different methods of operator training, *Ergonomics*, **1**, 39–50. (57)

BENSCHOTER, R. P. and CHARLES, D. C. (1957) Retention of classroom and television learning, *J. appl. Psychol.* **41**, 253–256. (64)

BILODEAU, E. A. and BILODEAU, I. McD. (1958a) Variation of temporal intervals among critical events in five studies of knowledge of results, *J. exp. Psychol.* **55**, 603–612. (28)

BILODEAU, E. A. and BILODEAU, I. McD. (1961) Motor-skills learning, *Ann. Rev. Psychol.* **12**, 243–280. (31, 93)

BILODEAU, I. McD. (1956) Accuracy of a simple positioning response with variation in the number of trials by which knowledge of results is delayed, *Amer. J. Psychol.* **69**, 434–437. (29)

BILODEAU, I. McD. and BILODEAU, E. A. (1958b) Transfer of training and physical restriction of responses, *Percept. mot. Skills*, **8**, 71–78. (48)

BRIGGS, G. E. and BROGDEN, W. J. (1954) The effect of component practice on performance of a lever-positioning skill, *J. exp. Psychol.* **48**, 375–380 (89)

BROADBENT, D. E. (1958a) *Perception and Communication.* Pergamon, London. (70, 97)

BROADBENT, D. E. (1958b) Effect of noise on an "intellectual" task, *J. acoust. Soc. Amer.* **30**, 824–827. (69)

BROADHURST, P. L. (1958) Emotionality and the Yerkes–Dodson law, *J. exp. Psychol.* **54**, 345–352. (9)

BRUCE, R. W. (1933) Conditions of transfer of training, *J. exp. Psychol.* **16**, 343–361. (104)

BRYAN, W. L. and HARTER, N. (1897) Studies in the physiology and psychology of the telegraphic language, *Psychol. Rev.* **4**, 27–53. (85)

BUGELSKI, B. R. (1942) Interference with recall of original responses after learning new responses to old stimuli, *J. exp. Psychol.* **30**, 368–379. (111)

BUGELSKI, B. R. (1956) *The Psychology of Learning.* Holt, New York. (87)

BUGELSKI, B. R. and CADWALLADER, T. C. (1956) A reappraisal of the transfer and retroaction surface, *J. exp. Psychol.* **52**, 360–366. (104)

CARR, H. A. (1921) The influence of visual guidance in maze learning, *J. exp. Psychol.* **4**, 399–417. (51, 55, 57)

CARR, H. A. (1930) Teaching and learning, *J. genet. Psychol.* **37**, 189–218. (43, 55)

CARTER, L. F. and SCHOOLER, K. (1949) Value, need and other factors in perception, *Psychol. Rev.* **56**, 200–207. (77)

CAVANAGH, P., THORNTON, C. and MORGAN, R. G. T. (1963) The AutoTutor and classroom instruction. 3. The British European Airways study, *Occup. Psychol.* **37**, 76–84. (133)

CHAPANIS, A., GARNER, W. R. and MORGAN, C. T. (1949) *Applied Experimental Psychology.* Wiley, New York. (63)

CLARK, L. V. (1960) Effect of mental practice on the development of a certain motor skill, *Res. Quart.* **31**, 560–569. (99)

CLARKE, A. D. B. and HERMELIN, B. F. (1955) Adult imbeciles: their abilities and trainability, *Lancet*, **ii**, 337–339. (84)

CLARKE, A. M. and CLARKE, A. D. B. (1958) *Mental Deficiency: The Changing Outlook.* Methuen, London. (87)

COLE, L. W. (1907) Concerning the intelligence of raccoons, *J. comp. neurol. Psychol.* **17**, 211–261. (39)

COLVILLE, F. M. (1957) The learning of motor skills as influenced by knowledge of mechanical principles, *J. educ. Psychol.* **48**, 321–327. (75)

CONKLIN, J. E. (1957) Effect of control lags on performance in a tracking task, *J. exp. Psychol.* **53**, 261–268. (27)

CONRAD, R. (1962) The design of information, *Occup. Psychol.* **36**, 159–162 (75)

COOK, J. O. (1963) "Superstition" in the Skinnerian, *Amer. Psychologist*, **18**, 516–518. (126, 132)

COOK, T. W. (1934) Studies in cross-education. III. Kinesthetic learning of an irregular pattern, *J. exp. Psychol.* **17**, 749–762. (107)

COOK, T. W. (1937) Whole versus part learning in the spider maze, *J. exp. Psychol.* **20**, 477–494. (88, 91)

COULSON, J. E. (Ed.) (1962) *Programmed Learning and Computer-Based Instruction.* Wiley, New York. (122)

COULSON, J. E. and SILBERMAN, H. F. (1959) Results of an initial experiment in automated teaching. In Lumsdaine and Glaser (1960). (126, 133)

CRAIG, R. C. (1956) Directed versus independent discovery of established relations, *J. educ. Psychol.* **47**, 223–234. (117)

CRAIK, K. J. W. (1947) Theory of the human operator in control systems .I. The operator as an engineering system, *Brit. J. Psychol.* **38**, 56–61. (13)

CRAM, D. (1961) *Explaining "Teaching Machines" and Programming.* Fearon, San Francisco. (128)

CROSSMAN, E. R. F. W. (1959) A theory of the acquisition of speed-skill, *Ergonomics*, **2**, 153–166. (84, 87)

CROWDER, N. A. (1960) Automatic tutoring by intrinsic programming. In Lumsdaine and Glaser (1960). (122, 129)

CROWDER, N. A. (1962) *The Arithmetic of Computers.* English Univ. Press, London. (128)

DALLETT, K. M. (1962) The transfer surface re-examined, *J. verb. Learn. verb. Behav.* **1**, 91–94. (104)

DAY, R. H. (1956) Relative task difficulty and transfer of training in skilled performance, *Psychol. Bull.* **53**, 160–168. (114)

DE NIKE, L. D. and SPIELBERGER, C. D. (1963) Induced mediating states in verbal conditioning, *J. verb. Learn. verb Behav.* **1**, 339–345. (69)

DE RIVERA, J. (1959) Some conditions governing the use of the cue-producing response as an explanatory device, *J. exp. Psychol.* **57**, 299–304. (76)

DEESE, J. (1958) *The Psychology of Learning.* 2nd Ed. McGraw-Hill, New York. (8)

DEESE, J. and HARDMAN, G. W. (1954) An analysis of errors in retroactive inhibition of rote verbal learning, *Amer. J. Psychol.* **67**, 299–307. (111)

DENNY, M. R., ALLARD, M., HALL, E. and ROKEACH, M. (1960) Delay of knowledge of results, knowledge of task, and the intertrial interval, *J. exp. Psychol.* **60**, (32)

DIGMAN, J. M. (1959) Growth of a motor skill as a function of distribution of practice, *J. exp. Psychol.* **57**, 310–316. (94)

DUKES, W. F. and BEVAN, W. (1952) Accentuation and response variability in the perception of personally relevant objects, *J. Pers.* **20**, 457–465. (77)

DUNCAN, C. P. (1958) Transfer after training with single versus multiple tasks, *J. exp. Psychol.* **55**, 63–72. (112)

ELWELL, J. L. and GRINDLEY, G. C. (1938) Effects of knowledge of results on learning and performance. I. A co-ordinated movement of both hands, *Brit. J. Psychol.* **29**, 39–54. (19)

ENGLISH, H. B. (1942) How psychology can facilitate military training—a concrete example, *J. appl. Psychol.* **26**, 3–7. (31)

ENGSTROM, J. and WHITTAKER, J. O. (1963) Improving college students' spelling through automated teaching, *Psychol. Rep.* **12**, 125–126. (134)

ENTWISLE, D. G. (1959) Ageing: effects of previous skill on training, *Occup. Psychol.* **33**, 238–243. (108)

EVANS, J. L., GLASER, R. and HOMME, L. E. (1959) A preliminary investigation of variation in the properties of verbal learning sequences of the teaching machine type. In Lumsdaine and Glaser (1960). (126)

FRANKLIN, J. C. and BROZEK, J. (1947) The relation between distribution of practice and learning efficiency in psychomotor performance, *J. exp. Psychol.* **37**, 16–24. (96)

FRY, E. B. (1960) A study of teaching machine response modes. In Lumsdaine and Glaser (1960). (133)

FULTON, R. E. (1945) Speed and accuracy in learning movements, *Arch. Psychol.* **41**, No. 300. (86)

GAGNÉ, R. M. and BAKER, K. E. (1950) Stimulus predifferentiation as a factor in transfer of training, *J. exp. Psychol.* **40**, 439–451. (77)

GAGNÉ, R. M., BAKER, K. E. and FOSTER, H. (1950) On the relation between similarity and transfer of training in the learning of discriminative motor tasks, *Psychol. Rev.* **57**, 67–79. (107)

GAGNÉ, R. M. and FLEISHMAN, E. A. (1959) *Psychology and Human Performance.* Holt, New York. (64)

GAGNÉ, R. M. and FOSTER, H. (1949) Transfer of training from practice on components in a motor skill, *J. exp. Psychol.* **39**, 47–68. (111)

GATES, A. I. and TAYLOR, G. A. (1923) The acquisition of motor control in writing by pre-school children, *Teach. Coll. Rec.* **24**, 459–468. (55)

GIBBS, C. B. (1951) Transfer of training and skill assumptions in tracking, *Quart. J. exp. Psychol.* **3**, 99–110. (113)

GLEITMAN, H. (1955) Place learning without prior performance, *J. com. physiol. Psychol.* **48**, 77–79. (40)

GOLDSTEIN, M. and RITTENHOUSE, C. H. (1954) Knowledge of results in the acquisition and transfer of a gunnery skill, *J. exp. Psychol.* **48**, 187–196. (24, 27, 30, 123)

GOSS, A. E. (1953) Transfer as a function of type and amount of preliminary experience with task stimuli, *J. exp. Psychol.* **46**, 419–428. (76)

Goss, A. E. and Greenfield, N. (1958) Transfer to a motor task as influenced by conditions and degree of prior discrimination training, *J. exp. Psychol.* **55**, 258–269. (79)

Green, E. J. (1962) *The Learning Process and Programmed Instruction.* Holt Rinehart, New York. (126)

Green, R. F. (1955) Transfer of skill on a following tracking task as a function of task difficulty (target size), *J. Psychol.* **39**, 355–370. (32)

Greenspoon, J. (1955) The reinforcing effects of two spoken sounds on the frequency of two responses, *Amer. J. Psychol.* **68**, 409–416. (69)

Greenspoon, J. and Foreman, S. (1957) Effect of delay of knowledge of results on learning a motor task, *J. exp. Psychol.* **51**, 226–228. (28)

Gunzburg, H. C. (1948) Experiments in the improvement of reading in a group of educationally subnormal boys, *J. ment. Sci.* **94**, 809–833. (84)

Harrison, S. (1958) Problems of piano playing, *Ergonomics*, **1**, 273–276. (81)

Haslerud, G. M. and Meyers, S. (1958) The transfer value of given and individually derived principles, *J. educ. Psychol.* **49**, 293–298. (117)

Hellebrandt, F. A. and Waterland, J. (1962) Indirect learning: the influence of unimanual exercise on related muscle groups of the same and opposite side, *Amer. J. phys. Med.* **41**, 45–55. (60)

Holding, D. H. (1959) Guidance in pursuit tracking, *J. exp. Psychol.* **47**, 362–366. (47, 51)

Holding, D. H. (1962) Transfer between difficult and easy tasks, *Brit. J. Psychol.* **53**, 397–407. (115)

Holding, D. H. and Macrae, A. W. (1964) Guidance, restriction and knowledge of results, *Ergonomics*, **7**, 289–295. (32, 48)

Holland, J. G. (1960) Teaching machines: an application of principles from the laboratory, *J. exp. Anal. Behav.* **3**, 275–297. (123)

Homme, L. E. and Glaser, R. (1959) Problems in programming verbal learning sequences. In Lumsdaine and Glaser (1960). (127)

Hoving, K. L. (1963) Influence of type of discrimination training on generalization, *J. exp. Psychol.* **66**, 514–520. (103)

Hovland, C. I. (1938) Experimental studies in rote-learning theory: III. Distribution of practice with varying speeds of syllable presentation, *J. exp. Psychol.* **23**, 172–190. (97)

Hovland, C. I. (1951) Human learning and retention. Chapter 17 in Stevens, S. S. (Ed.) *Handbook of Experimental Psychology*. Wiley, New York. (86, 117)

Howell, M. L. (1956) Use of force-time graphs for performance analysis in facilitating motor learning, *Res. Quart.* **27**, 12–22. (31)

Hunter, W. S. (1912) A note on the behaviour of the white rat, *J. anim. Behav.* **2**, 137–141. (39)

Jacobson, E. (1932) Electrophysiology of mental activities, *Amer. J. Psychol.* **44**, 676–694. (98)

Jahnke, J. C. and Duncan, C. P. (1956) Reminiscence and forgetting in motor learning after extended rest intervals, *J. exp. Psychol.* **52**, 273–282. (95)

Johnson, G. B. (1927) A study in learning to walk the tight wire, *J. genet. Psychol.* **34**, 118–128. (69)

Judd, C. H. (1908) The relation of special training to general intelligence, *Educ. Rev.* **36**, 28–42. (75)

Kaess, W. and Zeaman, D. (1960) Positive and negative knowledge of results on a Pressey-type punchboard, *J. exp. Psychol.* **60**, 12–17. (36, 51)

KARLIN, L. and MORTIMER, R. G. (1963) Effect of verbal, visual and auditory augmenting cues on learning a complex motor task, *J. exp. Psychol.* **65**, 75–79. (30)

KATONA, G. (1940) *Organizing and Memorizing.* Columbia Univ. Press, New York. (116)

KAY, H. (1951) Learning of a serial task by different age groups, *Quart. J. exp. Psychol.* **3**, 166–183. (37)

KAY, H. (1954) The effects of position in a display upon problem solving, *Quart. J. exp. Psychol.* **6**, 155–169. (57)

KAY, H., ANNETT, J. and SIME, M. E. (1963) *Teaching Machines and Their Use in Industry.* H.M. Stationery Office, London. (131, 134)

KELLER, F. S. (1943) Studies in international Morse code. I. A new method of teaching code reception, *J. appl. Psychol.* **27**, 407–415. (32)

KELSEY, B. (1961) Effects of mental practice and physical practice upon muscular endurance, *Res. Quart.* **32**, 47–54. (99)

KITTELL, J. E. (1957) An experimental study of the effect of external direction during learning on transfer and retention of principles, *J. educ. Psychol.* **48**, 391–405. (117)

KLAUSMEIER, H. J. (1961) *Learning and Human Abilities: Educational Psychology.* Harper, New York. (99)

KNAPP, B. N. (1961) A note on skill, *Occup. Psychol.* **35**, 76–78. (12)

KNAPP, B. N. (1963) *Skill in Sport.* Routledge, London, (89)

KNAPP, C. G. and DIXON, W. R. (1950) Learning to juggle. I. A study to determine the effects of two different distributions of practice on learning efficiency, *Res. Quart.* **21**, 331–336. (93)

KNIGHT, F. B. (1924) Transfer within a narrow mental function, *Elem. Sch. J.* **24**, 780–788. (116)

KNIGHT, M. A. G. (1963) The AutoTutor and classroom instruction. 2. The Royal Air Force study, *Occup. Psychol.* **37**, 68–75. (133)

KOCH, H. L. (1923) The influence of mechanical guidance upon maze learning, *Psychol. Monogr.* **32**, No. 5. (40, 42)

KRESSE, F. H., PETERSON, R. N. and GRANT, D. A. (1954) Multiple response transfer as a function of supplementary training with verbal schematic aids, *J. exp. Psychol.* **48**, 381–390. (75)

KRUEGER, W. C. F. (1947) Influence of difficulty of perceptual-motor task upon acceleration of learning curves, *J. educ. Psychol.* **38**, 51–53. (85)

LANER, S. (1954) The impact of visual aid displays showing a manipulative task, *Quart. J. exp. Psychol.* **6**, 95–106. (64)

LANER, S. (1955) Some factors influencing the effectiveness of an instructional film, *Brit. J. Psychol.* **46**, 280–292. (64)

LAVERY, J. J. and SUDDON, F. H. (1962) Retention of simple motor skills as a function of the number of trials by which knowledge of results is delayed, *Percept. mot. Skills*, **15**, 231–237. (29)

LAWRENCE, D. H. (1954) The evaluation of training and transfer programs in terms of efficiency measures, *J. Psychol.* **38**, 367–382. (108)

LAWSHE, C. H. and CARY, W. (1952) Verbalization and learning a manipulative task, *J. appl. Psychol.* **36**, 44–46, (79)

LEE, B. S. (1950) Effects of delayed speech feedback, *J. acoust. Soc. Amer.* **22**, 824–826. (28)

LEWIS, D., MCALLISTER, D. E. and ADAMS, J. A. (1951) Facilitation and interference in performance on the modified Mashburn apparatus:

I. The effects of varying the amount of original learning, *J. exp. Psychol.* **41,** 247–260. (110)

LEWIS, D., McALLISTER, D. E. and BECHTOLDT, H. P. (1953) Correlational study of performance during successive phases of practice on the standard and reversed tasks on the S A M complex co-ordinator. *J. Psychol.* **36,** 111–126. (112)

LEWIS, R. E. F. (1954) Consistency and car-driving skill, *Brit. J. indust. Med.* **13,** 131–141 (84)

LINCOLN, R. S. (1956) Learning and retaining a rate of movement with the aid of kinaesthetic and verbal cues, *J. exp. Psychol.* **51,** 199–204. (48, 52)

LINCOLN, R. S. and SMITH, K. U. (1951) Transfer of training in tracking performance at different target speeds, *J. appl. Psychol.* **35,** 358–362. (113)

LORDAHL, D. S. and ARCHER, E. J. (1958) Transfer effects on a rotary pursuit task as a function of final task difficulty. *J. exp. Psychol.* **56,** 421–426. (113)

LORGE, I. and THORNDIKE, E. L. (1935) The influence of a delay in the after-effect of a connection, *J. exp. Psychol.* **18,** 186–194. (29)

LOVELESS, N. E. (1962) Direction-of-motion stereotypes: a review, *Ergonomics,* **5,** 357–383. (6, 57)

LUCHINS, A. S. (1942) Mechanization in problem-solving. The effects of einstellung, *Psychol. Monogr.* **54,** No. 248. (116)

LUDGATE, K. E. (1924) The effect of manual guidance upon maze learning, *Psychol. Monogr.* **33,** No. 148. (44, 47, 51)

LUMSDAINE, A. A. (1959) Some issues concerning devices and programs for automated learning. In Lumsdaine and Glaser (1960). (121)

LUMSDAINE, A. A. and GLASER R. (Eds.) (1960) *Teaching Machines and Programmed Learning.* Nat. Educ. Assoc., Dept. Audio-Vis. Instruct., Washington.

LUNDIN, R. W. (1961) *Personality: An Experimental Approach.* Macmillan, New York. (21)

MACPHERSON, S. J., DEES, V. and GRINDLEY, G. C. (1948) The effect of knowledge of results on performance: II. Some characteristics of very simple skills, *Quart. J. exp. Psychol.* **1,** 68–78. (19)

MACRAE, A. W. and HOLDING, D. H. Method and task in motor guidance, *Ergonomics,* in press. (50, 52)

MAIER, N. R. F. and ELLEN, P. (1952) Studies of abnormal behaviour in the rat. XXIII. The prophylactic effects of "guidance" in reducing rigid behavior, *J. abnorm. soc. Psychol.* **47,** 109–116. (42)

MAIER, N. R. F. and KLEE, J. B. (1945) Studies of abnormal behaviour in the rat. XVII. Guidance versus trial and error in the alteration of habits and fixations, *J. Psychol.* **19,** 133–163. (41)

MANDLER, G. (1954) Transfer of training as a function of degree of response overlearning, *J. exp. Psychol.* **47,** 411–417. (111)

McALLISTER, D. E. (1953) The effects of various kinds of relevant verbal pretraining on subsequent motor performance, *J. exp. Psychol.* **46,** 329–336. (78)

McCORMACK, P. D. (1958) Negative transfer in motor performance following a critical amount of verbal pretraining, *Percept. mot. Skills,* **8,** 27–31. (79, 110)

McFANN, H. H. (1953) Effects of response alteration and different instructions on practice and retroactive facilitation and interference, *J. educ. Psychol.* **46,** 405–410. (110)

McGeoch, J. A. (1929) The influence of degree of learning upon retroactive inhibition, *Amer. J. Psychol.* **41**, 252–262. (84)

McGeoch, J. A. and McDonald, W. T. (1931) Meaningful relation and retroactive inhibition, *Amer. J. Psychol.* **43**, 579–588. (109)

McNamara, H. J., Long, J. B. and Wike, E. L. (1956) Learning without response under two conditions of external cues, *J. comp. physiol. Psychol.* **49**, 477–480. (40)

Melcher, R. T. (1934) Children's motor learning with and without vision, *Child Develpm.* **6**, 315–350. (47, 51)

Meredith, G. P. (1941) The transfer of training, *Occup. Psychol.* **15**, 61–76. (117)

Michael, D. N. and Maccoby, N. (1953) Factors influencing verbal learning from films under varying conditions of audience participation, *J. exp. Psychol.* **46**, 411–418. (65)

Miles, W. (1927) The two-story duplicate maze, *J. exp. Psychol.* **10**, 365–377. (57)

Miller, N. E. and Dollard, J. (1941) *Social Learning and Imitation.* Kegan Paul, London. (60, 61)

Miller, R. B. (1953) *Handbook on Training and Training Equipment Design.* U.S. Air Force, W.A.D.C. Tech. Report 53–136. (8, 17)

Morin, R. E. and Grant, D. A. (1955) Learning and performance on a key-pressing task as a function of the degree of spatial stimulus-response correspondence, *J. exp. Psychol.* **49**, 39–47. (57)

Munn, N. L. (1950) *Handbook of Psychological Research on the Rat.* Houghton Mifflin, Boston. (Harrap, London.) (40)

Münsterberg, H. (1892) *Beiträge zur Experimentellen Psychologie.* Siebeck, Freiburg. (81)

National Institute of Industrial Psychology (1956) *Training Factory Workers.* Staples, London. (2)

Naylor, J. C. and Briggs, G. E. (1963) Effects of task complexity and task organization on the relative efficiency of part and whole methods, *J. exp. Psychol.* **65**, 217–224. (89)

Neumann, E. and Ammons, R. B. (1957) Acquisition and long-term retention of a simple serial perceptual-motor task, *J. exp. Psychol.* **55**, 159–161. (69)

O'Brien, C. C. (1943) Part and whole methods in the memorization of music, *J. educ. Psychol.* **34**, 552–560. (87)

Osgood, C. E. (1949) The similarity paradox in human learning: a resolution. *Psychol. Rev.* **56**, 132–143. (104)

Pask, G. (1958) Electronic keyboard teaching machines. In Lumsdaine and Glaser (1960). (123)

Perry, H. M. (1939) The relative efficiency of actual and imaginary practice in five selected tasks, *Arch. Psychol.* **34**, 5–75. (99)

Pfafflin, S. M. (1960) Stimulus meaning in stimulus predifferentiation, *J. exp. Psychol.* **59**, 269–274. (76)

Poffenberger, A. T. (1915) The influence of improvement in one single mental process upon other related processes, *J. educ. Psychol.* **6**, 459–474. (104)

Porter, D. (1958) Teaching machines. In Lumsdaine and Glaser (1960), (122)

Porter, L. W. and Duncan, C. P. (1953) Negative transfer in verbal learning, *J. exp. Psychol.* **46**, 61–64. (108)

Poulton, E. C. (1952) Perceptual anticipation in tracking with two-pointer and one-pointer displays, *Brit. J. Psychol.* **43**, 222–229. (47)

POULTON, E. C. (1956) The precision of choice reactions, *J. exp. Psychol.* **51**, 9–17. (113)

PRESSEY, S. L. (1927) A machine for automatic teaching of drill material. In Lumsdaine and Glaser (1960). (120)

RAZRAN, G. H. S. (1940) Studies in configurational conditioning: V. Generalization and transposition, *J. genet. Psychol.* **56**, 3–11. (104)

RENSHAW, S. and POSTLE, D. K. (1928) Pursuit learning under three types of instruction, *J. gen. Psychol.* **1**, 360–367. (74)

REYNOLDS, B. and ADAMS, J. A. (1953) Effect of distribution and shift in distribution of practice within a single training session, *J. exp. Psychol.* **46**, 137–145. (95)

REYNOLDS, B. and BILODEAU, I. McD. (1952) Acquisition and retention of three psychomotor tests as a function of distribution of practice during acquisition, *J. exp. Psychol.* **44**, 19–26. (96)

RIPPLE, R. E. (1963) Comparison of the effectiveness of a programmed text with three other methods of presentation, *Psychol. Rep.* **12**, 227–237. (133)

RITCHIE, M. L. (1954) The Skaggs–Robinson hypothesis as an artifact of response definition, *Psychol. Rev.* **61**, 4–11. (108)

ROBINSON, E. J. (1927) The "similarity" factor in retroaction, *Amer. J. Psychol.* **30**, 297–312. (108)

ROCK, I. (1957) The role of repetition in association learning, *Amer. J. Psychol.* **70**, 186–193. (83)

RUBIN-RABSON, G. (1941) Studies in the psychology of memorizing piano music: VI. A comparison of two forms of mental rehearsal and keyboard overlearning, *J. educ. Psychol.* **32**, 593–602. (99)

SACKETT, R. S. (1934) The relation between amount of symbolic rehearsal and retention of a maze habit, *J. gen. Psychol.* **13**, 113–128. (98)

SEASHORE, R. H. and BAVELAS, A. (1941) The functioning of knowledge of results in Thorndike's line-drawing experiment, *Psychol. Rev.* **48**, 155–164. (16)

SEYMOUR, W. D. (1954) *Industrial Training for Manual Operations.* Pitman, London. (24, 90)

SEYMOUR, W. D. (1956) Experiments on the acquisition of industrial skills (part 3), *Occup. Psychol.* **30**, 94–104. (91)

SEYMOUR, W. D. (1959) *Operator Training in Industry.* Institute of Personnel Management, London. (2)

SHUCKER, R. E., STEVENS, L. B. and ELLIS, D. S. (1953) A retest for conditioned inhibition in the alphabet-printing task, *J. exp. Psychol.* **46**, 97–102. (95)

SIDDALL, G. J., HOLDING, D. H. and DRAPER, J. (1957) Errors of aim and extent in manual point-to-point movement, *Occup. Psychol.* **31**, 185–195. (6)

SIIPOLA, E. M. and ISRAEL, H. E. (1933) Habit-interference as dependent upon stage of training, *Amer. J. Psychol.* **45**, 205–227. (111)

SINGLETON, W. T. (1957) An experimental investigation of sewing-machine skill, *Brit. J. Psychol.* **48**, 127–132. (106)

SKAGGS, E. B. (1925) Further studies in retroactive inhibition, *Psychol. Monogr.* **34**, No. 161. (108)

SKINNER, B. F. (1954) The science of learning and the art of teaching. In Lumsdaine and Glaser (1960). (121)

SKINNER, B. F. (1961) *Cumulative Record.* Methuen, London. (20)

SMALL, W. S. (1900) An experimental study of the mental processes of the rat, *Amer. J. Psychol.* **11**, 133–165. (40)

SMITH, W. I. and MOORE, J. W. (1962) Size-of-step and achievement in programmed spelling, *Psychol. Rep.* **10**, 287–294. (126)

SMODE, A. F. (1958) Learning and performance in a tracking task under two levels of achievement information feedback, *J. exp. Psychol.* **56**, 297–304. (32)

STEEL, W. I. (1952) The effect of mental practice in the acquisition of a motor skill, *J. phys. Ed.* **44**, 101–108. (99)

SZAFRAN, J. (1951) Changes with age and with exclusion of vision in performance at an aiming task, *Quart. J. exp. Psychol.* **3**, 111–118. (14)

SZAFRAN, J. and WELFORD, A. T. (1950) On the relation between transfer and difficulty of initial task, *Quart. J. exp. Psychol.* **2**, 88–94. (113)

TAJFEL, H. (1957) Value and the perceptual judgment of magnitude, *Psychol. Rev.* **64**, 192–204. (77)

TAYLOR, D. W. (1943) Learning telegraphic code, *Psychol. Bull.* **40**, 461–487. (85)

TAYLOR, F. V. and GARVEY, W. D. (1959) The limitations of a "procrustean" approach to the optimization of man-machine systems, *Ergonomics*, **2**, 187–194. (6)

THORNDIKE, E. L. (1898) Animal intelligence, *Psychol. Rev. Monogr. Suppl.* **2**, No. 8. (39)

THORNDIKE, E. L. (1924) Mental discipline in high school studies, *J. educ. Psychol.* **15**, 83–98. (117)

THORNDIKE, E. L. (1927) The law of effect, *Amer. J. Psychol.* **39**, 212–222. (15)

TROWBRIDGE, M. A. and CASON, H. (1932) An experimental study of Thorndike's theory of learning, *J. gen. Psychol.* **7**, 245–260. (15)

TSAI, L. S. (1930) Gradual vs abrupt withdrawal of guidance in maze learning, *J. comp. Psychol.* **10**, 325–331. (40)

TWINING, W. L. (1949) Mental practice and physical practice in learning a motor skill, *Res. Quart.* **20**, 432–439. (99)

TWITMYER, E. M. (1931) Visual guidance in motor learning, *Amer. J. Psychol.* **43**, 165–187. (59)

UNDERWOOD, B. J. (1961) Ten years of massed practice on distributed practice, *Psychol. Rev.* **68**, 229–247. (93)

VAN BERGEIJK, W. A. and DAVID, E. E. (1959) Delayed handwriting, *Percept. mot. Skills*, **9**, 347–357. (28)

VANDELL, R. A., DAVIS, R. A. and CLUGSTON, H. A. (1943) The function of mental practice in the acquisition of motor skills, *J. gen. Psychol.* **29**, 243–250. (99)

VAN DUSEN, F. and SCHLOSBERG, H. (1948) Further study of the retention of verbal and motor skills, *J. exp. Psychol.* **38**, 526–534. (70)

VAN VALKENBURGH, NOOGER AND NEVILLE, INC. (1959) *Basic Electronics.* Technical Press, London. (118)

VERNON, M. D. (1951) Learning and understanding, *Quart. J. exp. Psychol.* **3**, 19–23. (63)

VERNON, M. D. (1953) The value of pictorial illustration, *Brit. J. educ. Psychol.* **23**, 180–187. (62)

VERNON, M. D. (1954) The instruction of children by pictorial illustration, *Brit. J. Psychol.* **24**, 171–187. (62)

VERPLANCK, W. S. (1955) The control of the content of conversation: reinforcement of statements of opinion, *J. abnorm. soc. Psychol.* **51**, 668–676. (69)

VON WRIGHT, J. M. (1957) A note on the role of guidance in learning, *Brit. J. Psychol.* **48**, 133–137. (51, 55)

WALLIS, D. and WICKS, R. P. (1963) The AutoTutor and classroom instruction: 1. The Royal Navy study, *Occup. Psychol.* **37**, 50–67. (124, 133)

WANG, G. H. (1925) The influence of tuition in the acquisition of skill, *Psychol. Monogr.* **34**, No. 154. (80)

WATERS, R. H. (1928) The influence of tuition upon ideational learning, *J. gen. Psychol.* **1**, 534–549. (75)

WATERS, R. H. (1930) The influence of large amounts of manual guidance upon human learning, *J. gen. Psychol.* **4**, 213–277. (45)

WATERS, R. H. (1931) The effect of incorrect guidance upon human maze learning, *J. comp. Psychol.* **12**, 293–301. (45, 52)

WATERS, R. H. (1933) The specificity of knowledge of results and improvement, *Psychol. Bull.* **30**, 673 (Abstr.). (32)

WATERS, R. H. and ELLIS, A. I. (1931) The relative efficiency of free and guided learning when equated in terms of time, *J. comp. Psychol.* **12**, 263–277. (45)

WELFORD, A. T. (1958) *Ageing and Human Skill.* Oxford Univ. Press, London. (86)

WELFORD, A. T., BROWN, R. A. and GABB, J. E. (1950) Two experiments on fatigue as affecting skilled performance in civilian aircrew, *Brit. J. Psychol.* **40**, 195–211. (69)

WHITELEY, G. (1963) Personal communication From Carnegie College of Physical Education, Leeds. (92)

WIENER, N. (1949) *Cybernetics.* Wiley, New York. (13)

WILLIAMS, D. C. S. (1956) Effects of competition between groups in a training situation, *Occup. Psychol.* **30**, 85–93. (9)

WILLINGHAM, W. W. (1958) Performance decrement following failure, *Percept. mot. Skills*, **8**, 199–202. (34)

WOLFLE, D. (1951) Training. Chapter 34 in Stevens, S. S. (Ed.) *Handbook of Experimental Psychology.* Wiley, New York. (112)

WYLIE, H. H. (1919) An experimental study of transfer of response in the white rat, *Behav. Monogr.* No. 16. (104)

INDEX